THE ROAD TO NOW

FROM TRAGEDY TO TRIUMPH

JESSICA SUMMERS

INTRODUCTION

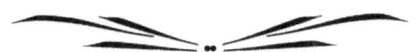

Life is a journey, a road filled with unexpected twists, daunting obstacles, and moments of profound clarity. "The Road to Now: From Tragedy to Triumph" is not just a recounting of events, but a testament to the human spirit's resilience, adaptability, and capacity for transformation.

Jessica's story is one of navigating through the deepest valleys of despair and ascending to the peaks of triumph. It is a journey marked by significant loss, searing pain, and overwhelming adversity. Yet, it is also a narrative of awakening, healing, and discovering an unshakable inner strength and purpose.

In these pages, you will find more than a memoir. You will uncover insights, lessons, and reflections that can illuminate your own path. This book is an invitation to explore how we can turn our darkest moments into our greatest opportunities for growth and empowerment.

As a speaker, consultant, and author, Jessica has dedicated her life to helping others find their peace, purpose, and power. Through personal stories, practical advice, and spiritual wisdom, she aims to guide you towards embracing your true self and living a life of authentic fulfillment.

Whether you are facing your own struggles, seeking inspiration, or looking to deepen your understanding of the human experience, "The Road to Now" offers a beacon of hope.

Welcome to your new beginning.

TABLE OF CONTENTS

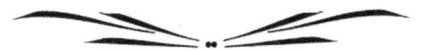

CHAPTER ONE

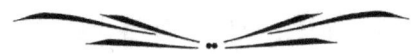

I started going out at night doing all the wrong things, but I was lost. I couldn't take it anymore. I don't even have the words to try to describe how lost I really was. It is a state of being that you have no rational explanation for, so you don't know where or what kind of help you need. I needed all the help in the world, but there was none. I now had only myself to rely on, and I didn't trust myself anymore. I didn't understand this diagnosis anymore, the medications, the side effects, the daily pain, and no longer knowing what was right or wrong. Nothing is the same from one day to another, and it is not easy to make any sense of what to do. It was a living hell that only I could see and feel. I had never in all my life been in a situation that I couldn't get myself out of, and the more I tried, the more I failed, the more intense my symptoms got. You lose track of what is your mental health and what is your physical health, both feeding off of each other in a negative way. I tried talking about it with my husband and family, but no one heard me; it was just complaining. I felt bad for feeling bad. I completely lost myself. Jokes of "you're old and broken"

made my already sad and depressed existence that much worse. I knew I wasn't the person I once was or the wife, the mother I wanted to be. I wasn't the person my husband had married, and I hated myself for it. I hated that I couldn't be there the way I wanted for my children and the way that they needed me to be. Don't think that doesn't play into my emotional well-being. Nightmares of my children calling for me, but mommy isn't there; she's sick. It got to the point that I would wake up every morning from a panic attack, wondering how bad the pain would be for that day. How would I feel? What kind of symptoms? What if someone needed something from me? Did I have the right medications? Did I have enough pain pills? Completely consumed. It was literal hell on earth. But I didn't really look sick, so what was I complaining about? You have no right to complain because you have everything you could ever want or need. I was married to the man I loved and had two beautiful baby girls; I was a Fashion Designer who owned and operated a boutique with another designer who was a friend of mine. On the outside, I had it all, and I really felt like I did too. I had more than I ever thought possible, but my health is dragging me down too slowly to notice how bad it really is until I can no longer get myself out of the hole I have dug for myself. I had lost the ability to care for myself, but I looked OK on the outside, so nobody heard me. I could say all I wanted about how I felt for the most; it was complaining that went in one ear and out the other. And if it wasn't ignored, then it was completely misinterpreted, which, in the long run, had me questioning my own sanity. I didn't know then or understand what I do now that no one really believed me. I couldn't understand why I was being spoken to the way I was or why I was being treated the way I was. I know now it's because nobody believed me. It took me to come full circle to understand that my husband and my family never believed me, or did they? I still can't totally wrap my head around it. I told everyone every chance I had that something was wrong with me, I was sick, and I was in pain. I waited and wanted so badly for someone to ask how I was feeling. I just wanted someone to really hear me, to have an answer. In the end, I just wanted someone to save me and take it all away. I was in daily pain, and I didn't have any real answers other than a different diagnosis every time I went to my doctor's appointment. My husband would get so angry with me, telling me that I didn't make healthy choices, and that it was my fault. And that was the very thing that was making me sink even further. It didn't matter what I did or did not do. The pain, nausea, diarrhea, constipation, and I had so many different diagnoses that I don't think my husband believed any of them. If I didn't look sick, I wasn't, and that was that. I was not allowed to be sick. If I was, it was due to the fact that I didn't take care of myself. I began to loathe myself as much as my husband did. I didn't want to make him unhappy, and I didn't want to be the person that he was telling me who I was. So, I started going out at night looking for answers that nobody else could give me. I would do anything to find some relief. I would do anything to keep my family. I would do anything just to be normal. I was told that I was selfish, but that was the very opposite of why I did what I did or where I ended up.

CHAPTER TWO

Everything had turned for the worse when we decided to leave San Francisco back to Sacramento. I didn't want to go but the choice wasn't mine to make. My oldest was about to start school and we didn't get into any of the schools that we wanted in San Francisco, so back to Sacramento to a school that was recommended to us by family. We had a friend that had a friend with a little rental property in the school district that we needed to be in, so just like that we were in the house and in the school that we wanted.

I'm still dealing with ab pains, nausea, and fatigue. Sometimes diarrhea, sometimes constipation, and what I didn't really know then what I do know now—Postpartum depression. I am basically fighting every day with either physical, mental, or emotional pain, and I have to start over now by trying to find a new doctor. I had been dealing with all of this since the birth of my second child. The last trimester to be precise. It was the opposite of my first pregnancy and delivery. The last trimester was in and out of doctors' appointments and ultrasounds. They were keeping an eye on her heart rate, fluids, and my blood pressure. I had labile blood pressure which means it would fluctuate from normal to really high. On my last appointment halfway through, my doctor said, "We're taking you across the street to admit you." They told me through the hustle and bustle that they were going to induce labor because they were worried that I was going to have a stroke. They admitted me, induced, but it still took what seemed like forever to have her. I had an epidural, but it only took on one side. They tried it a few times, but I still felt everything on one side of my body. I felt everything on one side, and the other side was like jelly. When she finally came into this world I remember laying there, in my head thinking, I don't hear her. Why don't I hear her crying? The nurses and my husband acted like it was no big deal, so I didn't think more about it. I know they had to resuscitate her. Torturous thoughts... I had to let go of all those epidural shots. You wonder what damage could have been done before she even came into this world.

After coming home from the hospital, I ended up having to go back. I had debilitating ab pains and after examination, they found placenta had been left behind. Again, thoughts that would later haunt me of what could have been done to my now brand-new baby. This is where I now see that this was the beginning of the end, and I never saw it coming nor would I have thought to look out for it. I left the hospital with antibiotics and pain pills and would have to come back time and time again for more. I ended up having to take more antibiotics for an overgrowth of bacteria from too many antibiotics. It would be hard to describe on my checkups sometimes because it felt like the pain was in other places and moving around and lower than it was originally. Sometimes they wouldn't find anything, but they would still send me home with pain pills and would make a different appointment with a different kind of doctor or specialist that would sometimes be months out. So, in the meantime, I tried dealing with whatever was going on and took my pain pills. What you don't know is that when you are in something like this that you have never been in before, you are unaware of the overall impact it has on your entire being. In between wait times of appointments, I would have to see my primary again because the pain was out of control, and the pills weren't working. I had ruptured ovarian cysts a few times, which I had never had before. I had to have an endometrial ablation. Somewhere in all of this, I had an appointment where they found that I had a hiatal hernia. I was given medication for this, which I believed to hurt my stomach more. I had been told time and time again that I needed the medication and was put back on it. Maybe it wasn't the medication itself, but in combination with the other medications and with the stomach issues I was having, that medication made it worse. Months had turned into years of undiagnosed, sometimes diagnosed, and sometimes a new diagnosis. H. Pylori was another new one that I had been diagnosed with more than one time and was given antibiotics and pain pills. I can't even really describe what that feeling was like. It just felt never-ending. If it wasn't one kind of pain, it was another. If it wasn't one kind of symptom, it was several all at once or something new. I was a nervous wreck, but I wasn't always allowed to show it. I didn't always show it because I was embarrassed, and I knew people were just tired of hearing about it. You couldn't get away from it. I don't know when the depression set in the way it did, but it was a slow insidious negativity that would eventually rule me. I had never been in a situation that I could not get myself out of, and I found myself completely helpless. And when you don't look sick, you are on your own. The words from my dad, "Nobody knows or can feel your pain" were a nightmare. It was true. I didn't have a fatal disease diagnosis; I didn't look sick. It didn't make sense to me then, but I know now that my husband did not believe me because he would not take no for an answer. I guess he thought I was being lazy or just trying to be difficult. I really don't know. He behaved as if I was putting him out and in turn, I would feel that way too. If we made plans, we went no matter how I was feeling. If we had a game that we were playing in, soccer or softball, we went no matter how I was feeling. The more I tried to do what was asked of me, the more pills I needed to take, the more anxiety I had, the more the darkness was taking over my life. My entire life now is just trying to keep up with keeping up. And I just kept doing it because I didn't know what else to do. It's way too late, and you're in too deep by the time you finally realize how far gone you really are.

When I think about it now, I know I always talked about my stomach pains, or how I was feeling, and it wasn't good. If I had run out of pain pills, I would ask whoever was around that had to take their own for whatever reason or had left over from a surgery or injury. You would be surprised at how many people take or have taken them and have some left over. I was just like those family members or friends who didn't think about addiction, the consequences, or any other problems in asking for pain pills. I was in pain, so I asked, and I received. Yet, nobody believed me or did they? I don't know. It was so confusing to me, it still is. If they never believed that I was really sick and in pain, then why would they give me pain pills? Now, of course, it's been a lot of years, and the answers to those questions no longer matter. But there was a time when those questions would keep me sick with the need to find the answers. The best thing I ever did, and if I could ever advise anyone, is to let go of the searching for the answers you will never receive. And in time they just don't and won't matter.

CHAPTER THREE

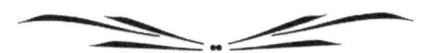

I'm commuting to my boutique two days a week. I drive there, let's say on Tuesday morning, work that day, stay the night at my mother-in-law's, work the next day, and then drive home that night. I know I've shared that I'm falling asleep trying to drive home and sometimes have to pull over to rest. I've talked to my husband and my family about these medications, and how I feel. I've said several times that I'm going to stop taking my medications because I don't know what's what and the potential side effects. I'm told on more than one occasion that I'm not a doctor and not to stop taking what has been prescribed to me. And just because there is a potential side effect, it doesn't mean I will have them. I'm well aware that both of these statements are true but that doesn't help me in the slightest. I wonder why these things are even being said to me. Am I not being taken seriously? I sometimes wonder if I'm not really feeling the way I think I am. Am I making these things up? But why do I actually feel the way that I say I do if I'm making it up? What kind of person does this? What is wrong with me? I feel like I'm losing my mind. I'm going crazy.

I had finally found a new doctor and we're starting from scratch. Well, kind of. I've told him what medicine I'm taking and for how long. I think I'm taking everything I was before. I must have had my medical files transferred too. Anyway, the doctor's appointments and the appointments for testing have started. In the meantime, I'm just trying to keep it together. I'm depressed and feel like I have no right to feel depressed, so I fake it as much as I can. Nobody hears me, or they don't believe me, so I try to pretend that everything is OK. I'm dying on the inside. I had to give up the boutique because I just couldn't do it anymore. I had to give up what I worked so hard to create. I'm dying on the inside. But I know that I need to direct my energy to my health and my family. By this time, in retrospect, I'm living on autopilot. I'm not even myself anymore. I'm just going through the motions. I'm in complete darkness with a forced smile on my face. Even though I've lost a ton of weight, I still don't look sick, I guess. I hear huffing and puffing from my husband every time I say I can't do this or that. I hate myself: I hate that I am no longer the person my husband married, and I absolutely hate myself for not being the mother that my daughters want and deserve. I'm not the mother that I want to be. I don't have any idea where to go or what to do to fix myself. What the hell is wrong with me anyway? I'm in another world, physically, mentally, emotionally, and spiritually.

I asked my husband to go to one of my doctor's appointments. I had told him how I was feeling. I told him that my medication wasn't working anymore. I told him that I felt like I was taking too much pain medication. Because when I started to feel OK, I didn't take as much, and then when the pain came back, it would be twice as bad. It would take more and more pills to even touch the pain, and it made the rest of my symptoms worse. I told my husband this as well as my doctor. My doctor preceded to tell me that I was habituated. I had never heard that before; basically, I was addicted. He says, "With the help of your husband, we will wean you off the pills and put you on methadone." This doctor on this appointment also diagnosed me with fibromyalgia. I had no idea what that was and the diagnosis alone just made me question what that had to do with my stomach. I was consumed. Now, anytime anyone tells me anything, it just swirls around in my head. Nothing registers or makes sense, and I can't make sense of that. What is being said to me is as if in another language. Why can't I make sense of what is being said to me? Or why is it being assumed that I should be able to understand what I cannot?

My husband helped me for one day. I guess it was too much; I was too much. He told me to get my shit together, but I didn't know what that meant. I tried going to talk to a therapist. And I think she was the only one who saw the unlucky position I found myself in. She was the only one who heard me when I told her I had uncontrollable stomach pains. Stomach pains so bad, it made me nauseous. Headaches so bad, they started in my shoulders, up my neck, over the back of my head to the front, and in the back of my eyes. When it was bad, it made me vomit. I told her I thought it was tension and stress for not getting real answers but only medications. She referred me to a psychiatrist; eventually, I got an appointment. I really need to preface that picking up the phone and making a next-day appointment for any doctor, or whatever specialist appointment that your MD refers you to or any mental health appointment takes a month if not longer to get. Sometimes you don't even know why you made the appointment in the first place because something new is going on. Or so much time has passed you can't remember what was going on at the time you made the appointment. And I need help that I don't even know what I need for. You give up and slide back on your way back to remind yourself to get up and take care of yourself. In the meantime, be a wife and mother and carry on as if everything is just fine and normal. Fake it until you make it. Or fake it because you don't want to make anybody else uncomfortable or angry with you.

I went and saw the psychologist that had been referred to me and he prescribed me valium. It wasn't the first time I had been prescribed benzodiazepines, and I hated them then as much as I did before. I had already lost myself and now I was going to add this stuff on top. But when you're desperate, you're desperate. I'm just trying to get right. I want this all to go away. I want my life back, and I want my family back. I am at arm's length from everyone; I'm there, but it's not me. Am I the only one that notices? That can't be right. I'm losing my mind. I don't even know if I'm seeing a doctor sometimes or if I'm just juggling medications. I hate the way I feel and I can't get away from any of it. I can't get away from myself. I'm running in circles around myself and digging myself ever deeper.

CHAPTER FOUR

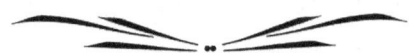

This is it. I have to do something else, something different. I tried going to another doctor. I take my husband to help me understand what's being said to me because I don't know what I'm missing. I lay on my stomach while I get shots in my neck that don't work or help me. My husband sits in the chair next to me on his phone; I'm on my own. I asked the doctor what fibromyalgia is and his opinion on that diagnosis. He tells me that doctors use that diagnosis when they can't find anything else to call it. I don't understand what is being said to me. He's also giving me his opinion on things that I didn't ask, and I just hear mumbling. I haven't understood what has been said to me for years. No one listens to a word I say, so it's really hard to listen to what is being said to me. It's as if we're not even speaking to each other. I seriously wonder sometimes if I have completely lost my mind, or if I'm in some twisted nightmare that I can't wake up from.

I stopped asking my husband to go to doctors' appointments with me after that. And somewhere in it all I quit going myself. I had said plenty of times and got the same response, so I finally just did it. I stopped taking all my medications. I thought I was doing badly before and didn't think it could get any worse. It got worse and even worse from there. I'm pretty sure that now I'm just looking for pain pills and no longer care about, well, anything.

I started going out at night looking for anything and anyone to save me. I'd go out to bars telling anyone who would listen to my sob story. I'm about as pathetic as a person can be. I just want someone to acknowledge me and what I'm saying. I wanted somebody to feel sorry for me, save me, and fix me. I'm throwing myself at anyone who will listen. One night out at a bar I meet someone, and we go back to an apartment where others are doing drugs. We're in the kitchen and he has the answer to all my problems. He shoots me up with heroin and just like that I have been saved. I pretty much right from the beginning started thinking about that and only that. I don't care about going to the doctor, I feel better than I have in years. I make it OK in my head that I'm doing this because I don't have to do a lot. I do just enough, so I can function and be normal. I don't have to juggle all of these medications to try to feel somewhat OK. I can now just do that without all these other added medications, and I feel better than ever. I can get out on the soccer or softball field with my husband. I can be there for my children. In my separation papers, it was said something like, "She must have been using while the girls were at school, which means she was still under the influence when she picked them up." My actions were made to demonize me when in my state of mind, I thought that that was all I had. I tried getting anyone and everyone's attention before and wasn't heard. And the only way I could get anybody's attention was by doing heroin. If I complained about how doctor-prescribed medication made me feel and fall asleep at the wheel, nobody heard me. What about being under the influence of all the medication that I've been trying to get someone to hear me say for years? I am a shell of myself, and I get told not to stop taking what my doctor prescribes me.

I made it OK, when, yes of course, I knew it wasn't OK, but I wanted to be normal. I wanted to be the woman my husband married, and I wanted to be the mother that my children wanted and deserved. You can't imagine the desperation. You finally get a break from the physical, mental, and emotional pain. How do you give that up when you have no other options? I wanted my life back. It is a fight with the devil that you can't ever win.

Sooner than later I become a slave to going to the person that shot me up, to get more. I can't get any unless I go through him. I have to buy it for the both of us, or he won't shoot me up. I don't know how to do it myself. The more I get sucked in, the more I start looking and finding my own supply, and I'm now shooting myself up. And not just in the arm, but anywhere I could find a vein. I sometimes muscle it (in my thigh or the back of my arm), so it will last longer. Remember, I'm not using to get high, I'm using to function and to be some kind of normal. How fast you lose yourself after selling your soul to the devil. I'm not sure how long I was doing it before, no matter how hard I tried to make it OK, I knew I had to stop. I had no idea what I was going to do. I made my already hopeless situation even worse. Trying to make sense of what you could not make sense of before, and now you're trying to wrap your head around the fact that you're a heroin addict. I'm in hell. I'm walking around what seems to resemble what I once knew to be my life, but this is no longer it. I'm lost. I'm sad, and I'm utterly heartbroken. What have I done?

CHAPTER FIVE

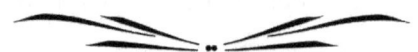

I really had tried everything I could. I even had drug dealers trying to help me find a time when I could get away for a weekend and wean myself off. It was September 2012; my mom had plans to go to Jamaica and wanted me to meet her and her husband there. I kept saying no. I probably said no in the beginning because I was a drug addict. All I could think about was that I couldn't find a way to use if I was away. It ended up that I would use that time as my weekend to "get away." I had met a dealer, and we became friends. If I remember correctly, she had either been a mortician or an EMT before she started selling drugs. I do remember that she said that she had seen too much death and pain, which mixed with her own hard-learned life experiences had become too much. We all can reach a point when enough is enough, and too much is too much. Next time you want to judge someone, I ask you to take a moment to ask yourself why and not automatically condemn. Start to wonder, and stop to ask questions. When we stay stuck in the world of absolutes, we limit ourselves and create suffering. We condemn ourselves enough without help from another.

So, the plan was that she was going to try and find me a fentanyl patch to wear, and I would take the bare minimum of heroin into Jamaica. I hid just a little bit in my underwear. So, I wore the patch and when I got there, the first thing I did was lose it the minute I dove into the water from the dock. The ocean can take all your worries away, but not that time. I tried not to panic and just focused on the fact that I still had a little bit of heroin with me, and it would be enough to wean myself off if I did it correctly. And I am on a mission. I'm trying to be as calm and calculated as I possibly can. Swimming, sunning, and staying mindful of what I'm doing and what I am to accomplish.

A lifeguard at one of the pools is eyeballing me, and I'm getting uncomfortable. I now believe wholeheartedly that you attract what you are putting out, where you are emotionally, mentally, and energetically. Even when I wasn't asking for it, it was coming to me. I go for a swim, come back to pick up my towel to dry off, and out come a couple of buds flying out. I threw my towel down and looked around, and there it was. The lifeguard is giving me a heads-up, an eyebrow lift, and a smile. Please no. Please just leave me alone. I go over to him to give it back, and he backs up shaking his head with his arms up, telling me he doesn't know what I'm doing. I start to turn around and he says in a low voice, "Just keep it." I'm so angry. I don't want or need anybody to come into my life to throw me off my plan. I've had this happen so many times before. Guys are just showing up in my life, worse off than me, wanting to save me. Yes, the exact words they used. And then getting called names because you don't want their help. It makes you want to give up. It makes you question the whole world and the people in it. It's like walking on a tightrope, trying to balance yourself until you can get onto some kind of solid ground. And when you get noticed that you're stumbling, in swoops the savior, just because he's a man, not because he can or is qualified. And you end up being the bitch.

The next day or two I'm trying to be as normal as I can around my mom, to do day trips to keep my mind occupied. What I had with me I would water down and snort it. Just so I have some in my system, so I don't go mad. Also, just because it's heroin, it doesn't mean that I am the picture depicted in the movies of what a heroin addict is. I'm doing it to be some kind of normal. I feel better and can function better than when I'm on all of those doctor-prescribed medications. By the day before my flight back home, I was on top of the world. I got this guy's pot back to him and had the strength to mean when I said to stay away and leave me alone. I didn't mention that he had asked me out a few times. He wanted to show me the real Jamaica and assured me that he and his wife had an open relationship. I didn't ask nor did I want any part of it. And I had weaned myself off and was going back home.

That day, the day before I was to go back home, I was out of control with excitement. What I mean is I was diving off the docks, doing backflips off this gigantic floaty thing in the water. Then I decided to get in on a soccer game on the beach with no shoes. I shouldn't be playing soccer with my shoes on, never mind without. Within no time, I kicked something or jam my toe; whatever I did, I broke it. I'm so bummed out. I can't believe what an idiot I am. Why couldn't I just be a normal, calm human being? The doctor comes to my room and just puts on something to try and protect it until I can get home. I get some pain pills but none to leave with. I get another wake-up call and a real taste of addiction because I don't care anymore about the work I did and now failed at. I can't wait to get home because I know I will get pain pills for my broken toe.

Trust me I know how bad it sounds. That's why it's important that I share it all. There is a really big difference between making a choice to do drugs and addiction. You no longer have a choice when it comes to addiction. I tell you this from my experience in both. I don't want to misrepresent myself. I had a time in my life in my twenties and before I was married that if drugs were around I would most likely have done them. Not heroin, but just about everything else. I won't go down a list of things because that isn't the point. My point is, at that time in my life, I made choices and if I felt like it, I would. And if I didn't feel like it, I wouldn't. And if I did, maybe I would feel it the next day a little bit, but not enough to make me spend my whole day looking for more. At that time, I was able to end relationships if drugs were being abused. I always craved normalcy in my life.

Not totally sure what comes next. I know I have another doctor I am seeing. I think he knows about my stomach issues, fibromyalgia, or whatever else is going on. I'm pretty sure this is the doctor I saw about my broken toe and another time when I tore a rotator cuff playing softball. By this time, I'm about half and half. Half trying to get help, half not giving a shit anymore. Because of the state I'm in physically and mentally, I'm just an accident waiting to happen.

I'm not 100% sure that the bits and pieces I'm telling you about go in the order that they happen. I just know they happened. I know they happened because they became nightmares that I could not shake without all the help that I ended up getting.

I'm back to using again. Of course, I'm back to using. My situation isn't just about weaning myself off heroin. I need help and not just for the drugs. I'm sick in every possible way. I'm just going around and around in circles. I'm completely out of control. I want everything to go back to normal, but I don't even know how. I can't make sense of anything. I want things to be normal, but I'm also terrified of the pain and the darkness. You can't even call it depression anymore. It's more than that. It is a darkness outside of this world and our understanding. It follows you in your waking hours and finds you in your sleep. You can't run, and you can't hide. No one can hear you, and no one wants to listen. It breaks your heart with the thought of even thinking about sharing such ugly, dark negativity, so you keep it to yourself. Everything ugly in this world is racing through your head and you can't stop it. The pains in my stomach consumed me with anxiety about how bad it would get and how it would affect the things I had to do that day. I would get mad at myself if I couldn't get it together because I knew I was letting others down. The worse I felt, the more drugs I took, the more I hated myself for what I was doing. You hate yourself so much that you want to take your own life to ease the pain, but you don't because you deserve to feel that pain. The Devil in your ear is laughing at you for any kind of positive self-talk you try to give yourself.

I am consumed every waking and sleeping hour with what I'm going to do. It's impossible. You don't know who you are or what to trust. The darkness inside that no one sees keeps it like that to make sure you are on your own. If I get help for drug addiction, then I have to deal with the physical issues that got me to this place to begin with. And my mental health has got me in its clutches. When you're in it, you can't make sense of what kind of help to ask for. You don't really think you deserve it either. Stigma is a killer, coming from you and others. And if nobody believed me before, why would they now—they won't. I'm going to snap.

I had no options left and I felt myself slipping even more. I think it's about two weeks before I had my break. I was sitting in this roach-infested apartment, at the table in the kitchen. Others were in the living room, but I had no idea what they were talking about, and they barely noticed that I was even there. I bought some heroin. I bought enough to do some there and have enough for the rest of the day and the next day. This time, without really paying attention to what I'm doing, I cook it all up. My head is spinning and I can't stop it long enough to answer any of the millions of questions that are going around in my head. I'm trying to get myself together for a second. I can't stop thinking about my husband and my family, my children. I'm in complete agony. I know I have to ask him for help but I am absolutely terrified. I think he will understand. But then, I think of the things he has said to me. I know he will understand, right, because he knows I'm sick. He's been to the doctor with me. But no, he won't understand, since he told me to get my shit together. But no, he comes with me to pick up my doctor's prescribed medication. But. I'm going to snap, nothing is making sense. I'm just sitting there, leaning down with my arms across my legs staring at the puddles of tears on the kitchen floor. Spinning, spinning, crying, screaming, and my whole body feels it, but no sound comes out. I feel like I'm underwater and drowning. This pain is not of this world. I pulled the plunger up and filled up the syringe. I'm crying when I put the needle in and ask God, "Why would you want me to suffer so badly?" I injected the whole thing, which should have killed me or at very least knocked me out. But I heard him, he said, "I don't." I heard it and I felt it in my entire being. I don't know how I was able to do it, but I dried my eyes, got up, and left. I got up and left. I never went back there again. I got up, walked out, and drove home. I did three times the amount that I usually did, and I got up and walked out. I was going to be OK...right.

CHAPTER SIX

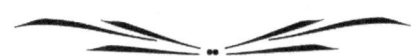

I'm on a mission. A mission to do what and how I have no idea. But I left that apartment, I was different. Something was different. God talked to me. I didn't need to hide, ashamed, from him anymore. I have to tell my husband. I must tell on myself. The thought makes me sick, but a small voice tells me he will understand. He will understand and know that I need help. He will understand how I got to where I did. Actually, I don't have a real understanding of anything, and I don't think he will either. I'm scared to death. But God saved me. But how and what am I going to say and do? I did my best and look where I ended up. I needed serious help. Those thoughts that he would understand also spun around with everything evil, ugly, and dark. But I know if I don't throw myself to his feet, I will die. The Devil is in my ear laughing and telling me I'm not worth it, and it's either life as I know it now or die. That battle lasted for days.

I had heard someone talking about being on a 72-hour hold in a mental institution for shooting too much meth, so in my not-so-rational mind, I thought that's what I needed to do as well. I need to be locked up because I am a monster, and I can't be trusted. So, I got some meth and started shooting that, which I had never done before. I had stopped taking all of my medication a while back, and now I'm shooting meth. I'm desperate. I'm lost in a black hole with no way out. And nobody even knows I'm missing.

The night before I said anything to my husband we were lying in bed. He was asleep, and I cried for hours. I knew what I was going to do, and I was battling the devil at the same time. It is a place in time and space that has no explanation. It is an event outside of human understanding. Heartbroken and scared to death, spiritual warfare. After hours of just laying there crying I got up and went into the first bedroom and picked up my oldest child, laid her down next to her dad, then went and got my little one and laid her down. All three of them were facing my way and I cried all night. Something was going to happen that would change the lives of all of us. I don't think my thoughts about what was to come are really rational, but none of this is. My mind, body, thoughts, and everything are pulling in different directions. The next morning my husband wakes up and looks at me with a strange look on his face and wonders what the girls are doing in our bed. The girls wake up confused with smiles on their faces for being in mommy and daddy's bed. Within seconds the house was in its loud controlled chaos, everyone getting ready for the day. I just lay in bed watching. I don't remember if my husband asked why the girls were in our bed or not. I just remember him saying, more than once, be ready right when I get home, we're leaving. We have Kings' tickets. My heart is racing with every word that is coming out of his mouth. I am literally dying inside, and he says we're going to a Kings' game. The fact that he can't or refuses to see how sick I am makes my already challenged thought process slip, slip, slip. Out the door they go, be ready he says one more time, I feel like I'm going to vomit, the door slams shut, the car drives off, and then silence. No one there besides me, and the Devil that dances around me and laughs at me every time I tell myself, I'm going to be ok. I pace, fidget, and wait. I'm going to be OK, I try to tell myself. No, I'm not. Oh my God, please help me. I'm going to lose my mind. Everything hurts. Please God help me. I'm losing my mind. I can't get away from any of it. I'm actually shooting up meth and begging God to let me hit a vein. I can only say that this is what it looks like to be under the control of the Devil. And in the back of my mind, I still think I need to be locked up, and this will get me there. I need to be locked up, I need to be under lock and key. I'm a monster. The anxiety attacks one after another with every thought of what's to come when they get back. I'm in fear of the fear. I already can't understand this darkness and how I can make such things up in my head. If it's this bad, how much worse could it get? That is the most terrifying thought that keeps me stuck every time I even think about doing the right thing, whatever that means.

I hear the car doors slamming shut one after the other and the alarm being set. I have to go lay down in bed because I feel like I'm going to pass out. The girls are in their rooms, and he comes into ours. He sees me on the bed and says something about not being ready or telling me to get ready. Something along those lines of we are still going, so you better get up. I don't know if I said it or if I was thinking it, but if I get up, I'm going to die. My heart is racing so fast that I feel like I'm going to pass out. I sit up and one word after another comes out. I basically tell him that I'm the worst person on the planet, that I'm a lying, cheating, stealing, junkie piece of shit, and so on. I don't even know all the things that I was saying. He kept asking me questions that I didn't have the answers to. I don't understand some of the questions or why I'm even being asked, so I just said yes. I said yes to things I did, I wasn't doing or didn't do. I just needed him to hear that I was in trouble and I needed help. I'm in the worst possible position ever. Why am I being asked these questions? I didn't want to hurt any more than I already had and I never wanted to hurt anybody else. I didn't know how to ask for help anymore, and the truth didn't work.

I remember him telling me to get my shit together among some other loud, angry words. And he tells me how he does everything for me, and how well he treats me. What does that have to do with me being sick? I don't understand again. He grabs the girls and leaves. I didn't move, I was frozen in time. I don't understand that I don't understand that I don't understand. It must have been about an hour later when my dad and stepmom came flying through the door with terror and confusion in their eyes. My heart breaks into even smaller pieces. We went to their house. I think I might have packed some things before we left. I think I was there for a day, three, four, or more. I'm not really sure. This is where stopping taking my medications and doing heroin, and starting to shoot meth all collide.

It seems like every waking moment I'm being told to go to sleep, but I'm too scared to sleep. I've slipped even farther. Years later I went through my old writings of that time. I have a notebook of me writing notes to myself saying it's OK to go to sleep. The words are written around in a circle as if I'm turning the notebook after every word I write. Don't ask me why. I tell myself that I am with my dad and stepmom and that they can be trusted, and they want me to go to sleep. It's just for now, I promise myself I will wake up. Every time I lay down, the shadows on the walls are too much. I jump up and freak out my dad and stepmom again. I know I had said that I needed to talk to my Godmother. Another person I am sure I scared the shit out of. I don't remember the conversation, but I do remember saying that I thought I was being tested. She's a very devout Italian Catholic. I think that's why I needed to call and say those words. I guess I thought she would be the only one who would understand those words. I don't know what I'm thinking exactly but she is the only person that I know that is really a religious person. Like I said I don't know what I thought I was going to do or get out of calling her and having that conversation. I was just outside of my understanding kind of afraid. It was out of this world kind of fear. I had never felt so alone in all of my life.

We've been to the ER a couple of times, and they sent me home again with a "one day at a time" pep talk. We've been to the hospital in the middle of the night, the afternoon, and morning. We're all over the place. One morning, I don't remember getting there, but we are in another Emergency room. I just know that my stepsister is in the waiting room with us this time. Back in the waiting room for I have no idea how long, I'm having convulsions or something. It's like I'm having some kind of seizure or something. The next thing is that I'm sitting in the back, maybe getting my blood pressure checked. I don't know how I got from having convulsions to sitting in the back. It was total chaos back there: people everywhere and loud. For what feels like a minute or two. Everything in the room stops. The people were blurred into one and then into the next. You couldn't tell what started or ended where. It was like a photo when you put your camera on a long exposure to pick up the streak of lights. I was the only figure there and sat there in silence. Someone bends down. I can't make anything out about them other than a figure and their eyes. The blurred figure bends down and looks into my eyes. Their eyes were bright and light. They told me not to worry and that we all go through it or will go through it. I'm not totally sure. And then everything went back to loud hustle and bustle. I got up and we walked out. I've asked my stepsister several times if she remembers that and if she had the same experience as I did. She had an experience, but I don't know if it was the same as I did. To me, I had another out-of-this-world experience. It is an experience that you really don't share with others or even try to explain. I just knew I was going to be OK. With no evidence of that from this world, I still had a knowing that I was going to be OK. I still, however, had no idea what this world and the people in it had in store for me. It's a good thing that I wasn't shown what it would take or how long it would take because I wouldn't have been able to wrap my human mind around it. I would have never been able to make sense of it. I wouldn't have been able to understand. I just had a newfound faith and knew that was going to get me through, no matter what. The beginning of my spiritual awakening and journey outside of anything that I had ever known before.

This must have been the last of the ER excursions because the next image I have is the ER, different than the one before. And I could feel myself slipping. I knew that I was losing my mind and my ability to control whatever was going to come next. I didn't want to scare my family any more than I already had. Believe it or not, you get little flashes of reality through this whole thing, and you know exactly what you have done and the remorse that comes with it. It's unbearable. It is an all-consuming guilt and sadness that kills. These are the feelings and emotions that lead to people taking their own lives. It's too much, it's unbearable. I need nothing more than love and understanding at this moment, but I don't deserve it. Please God have mercy. And I must get my dad out of here before it's too late. I'm going to a place that I don't know if I'll come back from. I don't want my dad to see this. I'm so sad, but I think I said something mean to get him out of there. I know I will battle the Devil himself sometime very soon with no one there to help me. I'm in a place where I have no choices, and I don't matter and no longer exist. I'm slipping.

My next memory is of me walking down a hallway. Nothing looks familiar. We keep stopping waiting to unlock a door. The last door unlocked, and I walked into an open room. The nurses station in front of me. Somebody is talking, and I don't know what they are saying. Nothing makes sense, but I realize I'm in a mental institution. How I got there or what happened at the ER before that, I have no memory whatsoever. After realizing where I was, I was grateful and thought I was right where I needed to be. This is where I needed to be, under lock and key and supervised 24/7. These were the people and the place that was going to help me. I didn't know it then, but I also needed to get out of the environment that I was in. I knew something wasn't right, something wasn't right besides just myself, but I didn't know what it was. It took me years of therapy before I could put a name on and understand what a gaslighting narcissist was.

I was there for a total of 17 days, but I can only remember a few instances, and I don't know what happened when. I just have a memory, but it doesn't go with the next memory. Or I guess it does, it's all the events that I can remember while being in a mental institution for 17 days. One of the first memories I have is that I'm in a room with two beds. I have a roommate. She's sitting on her bed with her back up against the wall. I'm standing across from her. I can't remember what we were talking about. I do remember her laughing. From where I'm standing, I can see the door to our room, it's open. I see these two bouncers-looking guys, and they are on a mission. They are marching in my direction. My heart starts racing because I'm looking around and can't figure out where they're going. My heart drops, they are there for me, and I don't have any idea why. One on each side of me, and they're dragging me out of my room. My roommate is yelling at me, "What did you do?" I swear to her I have no idea, and I really don't. I'm scared to death. My mind is racing. I'm questioning myself. What have I done? I'm crying and asking them what I did and where they are taking me. Nothing, no answer. My roommate and I are both yelling and crying, me asking what I did, and she asking me what I did, but neither one of them says a word. And out the door they drag me.

I never got an explanation as to why, what, or where. I just remember waking up and I'm in a pitch-black room, lying on a bed. I can't see my own hand before my eyes, so I feel around. I'm terrified. It felt like it took me hours to extend my arm out. I was consumed with fear and what I might touch or run into. I don't know where I am, and my imagination is dark, ugly, and terrifying. My next memory is that I'm in my bed in the room with my roommate, and I don't have a clue how I got there. I don't know where I was before, and I don't know how I got to where I am now. I rolled over and my right hip was too sore to lay on. My roommate tells me that they give you a shot if you are being non-compliant. Non-compliant for what, for not being OK for forcibly being removed from my room. It wasn't long before my happiness to be there turned into more questioning of the madness. You learn really quickly that if you have any sense at all, sometimes it's out of your control and you don't, but when you do, you say and do whatever they tell you to. Talk about maddening. If you aren't already questioning your sanity, this place will push you there. And the people that work there are just as bad with the way they talk, openly without a thought of how it might affect the people who are there. I don't know the role of this person I'm going to tell you about. It's not a doctor but one of the "staff" that work there "to help you." She tells a fellow "staff" that she was going to meet her mom for lunch and had to meet her outside. She says that her mother is still too afraid to come to her place of work. Then proceeded to say, "I tell my mom it's like working at a zoo, you know which cages you can go into and which ones to stay out of." And this was the place that I was trying to get into to get help. This was the place where out of complete desperation, I thought that I would be safe. I'm an animal at the zoo, not a human being who needs help.

One night or early morning, probably around 2 or 3 am, I'm walking up and down and around the halls, and I keep being told to go to bed. "Go to bed, Jessica", over and over. Not are you OK, or can I do something for you? Go to bed! It's the lady behind the nurse's station. I don't know what her role is there though. I notice that as I'm walking around I'm rubbing my stomach and I'm having really bad ab pains. I don't get it. I thought I was lying. I thought I made it all up to get drugs. From all the yelling and what had been said to me, I thought I had been lying and making it all up. I had been told what a terrible person I was amongst other things, so I thought I was making it up. I don't even know what to do with my thoughts, yet again. How can I be feeling something physically that I made up? I'm trying to just keep it together. I hate going to bed in one room and waking up in another without knowing anything in between. Or waking up sore and having horrible thoughts running around in my head wondering what happened and why I got another shot in my side.

I drop to my knees because I can't stand it, I can't stand the pain. It's my stomach. An ambulance gets called and I'm taken to emergency. I just remember being there in a bed with IVs in my arm. This time it was diverticulitis or colitis. When I get sent back to the psych hospital I also get sent with a prescription for antibiotics and pain pills. Are you kidding me? This is exactly how this all started, but still, nobody hears me and disregards every word out of my mouth. Because of my actions, because I am now a mentally ill drug addict, I no longer have a voice. In fact, I have been diagnosed with bipolar disorder. I try to argue that diagnosis because I'm not. And when I have reactions to medications, they up the dosage. I tried talking to my husband about it, and he told me that I'm either bipolar or a bad person. And then proceeded to tell me that I was telling friends of ours that I was bipolar. No, I didn't. I never said that, why would I? I'm questioning MYSELF again. And I'm really starting to fear my husband. Why would I tell anybody that? I wouldn't, I didn't. I'm totally questioning my entire reality.

It took me years to get anybody to hear me. That diagnosis followed me everywhere I went. In fact, in the beginning, when I was still fighting to get back to my family, I tried to fit into what I was being told. I took the medication even though it made things worse. I just wanted my family back; I just wanted some kind of normalcy. I tried to be bipolar because I didn't want to be a bad person. I mean, I guess I really was one or the other if what I was saying was a lie, but it wasn't a lie, or was it? I have a hard time understanding how I can make up such pain if I'm lying. And if I try to bring it up I get told to "stop living in the past." What in the hell does that mean? I'm living in this right now. I thought I was the mentally ill one. What in the hell is being said to me?

I could see how stigma and what people think they know about mental health or addiction have nothing to do with the truth. Because of where I was and what I had done, my words meant nothing. I was a crazy, worthless drug addict. No one wanted to listen to me that I couldn't and shouldn't be on anti-psychotics, that they made things worse. I had been diagnosed, with the help of my husband. But I knew that my behavior was due to no food, no sleep, chronic pain, major depression, anxiety, not understanding any of this diagnosis, or the lack thereof, medications and their side effects, way too many drugs, and no one listening to a word I had to say!! I still don't really know or understand my husband's behavior. Even writing these words right now brings up uneasy feelings and mixed emotions. I had to stop thinking about the answers to those questions because they had no answers. And those are the questions that literally drove me to insanity. I had to surrender those questions and only then did I get any peace to even start the smallest bit of healing and recovery. I had to be OK with not having the answers to that. In the end, I believe that saved my life. First, I had to heal enough and do the work to understand that I needed the help for me and in my way. I had to heal the wounds that were there, not the ones that were being told to me that I had. I had to finally start doing it for myself. Only then did the real healing begin.

I don't even know what medication they are giving me at this time, I'm just being as compliant as I can be, I don't want any more shots in my butt or to wake up someplace else without knowing how I got there. The days that I remember are always different from the last ones I remember.

On the days that I do have some kind of sense, I give myself pep talks in the bathroom mirror. I remind myself that no matter what I will get myself out of there. Another day I'm in a different room again. There is only one bed, so I have no roommate. I can barely move, and I've had my head hanging in a garbage can and throwing up for what feels like days. At the worst of it, I barely had a voice from throwing up so much, but I tried to cry out for help. No one came. I just lay there freezing and throwing up. Someone did finally bring me some kind of meal replacement shake or something. I finally have enough energy to get up and go to the shower that I believe is the door right next to mine, maybe two doors down but not farther. I had to walk with my back against the wall to keep myself from falling. I had nothing left. I turned the shower on to an almost intolerable heat and sat on the floor.

I'd lean up against the wall unless I had to throw up. I didn't have anything to throw up so it was more like dry heaving over the top of the shower drain. I got a knock on the door after I had been in there for too long, and I said I would be right out. I was in no hurry. When I did finally have the strength to get up, I tried to use the wall and the shower curtain to help get me up. I got up part of the way and the shower curtain ripped until I was all the way back down. I landed across the step into the shower on my side. I could barely move. I was hurt and freezing and just wanted to get back to my bed. I put half my clothes on and wrapped myself in the shower curtain. I made it back to my room and threw myself on the bed with a shower curtain and all. I was so cold and had no energy to do anything but that. I wasn't laying there long when a nurse walked in and, surprisingly, said, "Jessica, what are you doing?" I'm cold, and I'm crying. She helps me out of the shower curtain and gets some dry clothes on me. I lay there for a lifetime until I woke up somewhere else.

I do remember this nurse from something else that had happened. I'm in the main hallway, and I think I had just threatened her and her children whom I don't even know that she has. I don't know what I said, I just came to, if you will, right at the end of what I was saying, and I just know that it wasn't nice. I don't know where this is coming from or why. I dropped to my knees crying, begging her to forgive me, that I have children of my own, and I would never say anything or do anything to hurt hers. She comes over and helps me up. "It's OK, Miss Jessica, let's get you back into your room." It's the same room where I would find myself wrapped up in a shower curtain. She helps me into bed and tells me she'll be right back and just stay in bed and relax. I did. I waited for her to return because I also wanted to show her pictures of my girls and show her I was a mother too. And again, to forgive me for whatever words that came out of my mouth. She comes in with some water, crackers, and a stack of papers. It's a few pages of medications, and she shows me what I'm on, what it's for, and what side effects to watch out for. It took me months, maybe even years after getting out of there to really understand what she was doing for me. I couldn't understand my own thoughts or the lack of them, so I really had no idea or understanding that she was trying to help me. I had another nurse I remember meeting right around the time when I first got there. She was always nice and friendly. She was a bit older, and I remember her telling me she was finishing up her schooling, what kind I don't know. I'm sure it had something to do with mental health or she wouldn't have been there asking me these questions. She came to me one day and asked if it was OK if she followed me around and if we could talk. We did talk several times about what I don't know, but they were always nice and friendly conversations. I know I was getting close to my discharge date, and she had followed me around and kept telling me that she really wanted to see me before I left. "Sure, of course," I remember telling her even though I still didn't really know why. I was still in a place where I would respond in a nice, coherent way, but I didn't know how to follow through with it. I'm just going through the motions without any thought behind it. I just had the words but I did not know how to do whatever I said I would. In my discharge paperwork, it said that I was disabled and unable to care for myself. She has "no insight into her current situation." But those were just words to me that I really didn't understand any of it. And nobody else read that paperwork either.

So, she found me one day and asked if we could go sit down somewhere and have a talk. We sat down, and she handed me these brightly colored cutouts of paper dolls in dresses. Didn't make sense at that time. She had tears in her eyes, which I didn't understand either at the time. She gave me paper doll cutouts one at a time. On one side was the name of a medication that I am on and on the other were potential side effects. I thanked her and took them home. It took years of therapy for me to understand after remembering these events what any of them meant. I know that these nurses were trying to help me the best they could with what they had. I know that the little dress cutouts were to help remind me of who I was as a fashion designer. And that because of the conversations that we had had she knew that I needed help remembering who I was and that the medications I was given weren't what I needed to be on. I wasn't bipolar...

I'm pretty sure I went to my dad's first. I do remember him driving me to an outpatient program a few days a week, I think. The outpatient program is a step down from the psychiatric hospital. It's a smaller place, with fewer people. Two groups were going on simultaneously throughout the day with periodic one-on-one therapy sessions and family meetings or therapy. I don't really remember how or what those were about. I only remember one with my husband being there, and my therapist just told me that he was really mad. We had more conversations and tried to figure out why he was so mad instead of giving me the help that I needed. Maybe that's what he was trying to tell me, that was the help I needed. I wasn't ever going to heal if I had someone who was constantly mad and yelling at me. And I would heal and finally figure it all out years later far removed from my marriage. I saved all of the paperwork I got from all these places for later because I didn't understand most of what was being said to me at the time. I don't understand but my family keeps asking me questions as if I am to know. And if I don't have the answer, I get yelled at. I'm told that I'm "a fucking liar."

One day in the hallway my psychiatrist came up to me and asked how long I'd had the rash across my chest. I didn't even notice I had a rash. On some of these medications, I didn't notice most things, I barely remembered my own name. But because of the rash, he took me off one of my medications immediately. I looked at the paperwork years later, and I saw that the medication had a black box warning about being potentially fatal and to watch out for rashes. It also had in the doctor's notes that my dad had called a few times saying that I had a lot of stomach pains. I ended up having to leave the program because I went into the hospital due to my ab pains. That was definitely one of the more helpful places I had been. I had tried doing these things alone before and failed. You need help to get help. Before, I had been yelled at if I had made an appointment but then forgot to go. I couldn't keep track of anything. And forgot most things. I just wanted to run. I didn't want to abandon anyone like my children had been told. I wanted to run to get help. Being at a place where you have the one-on-one and group sessions, and a psychiatrist ready and there for you, at that time made all the difference in the world. We would all like to say that family would be there to help us, but they don't know how, and they don't know that they don't know. And it's also called stigma. We all have been so brainwashed into this black-and-white, right-and-wrong way of thinking that we are unaware that we are a huge part of the problem. And I know what I'm talking about because I thought the same way until I had gone through it. That's one of the biggest problems itself because of the stigma people think they have a license to give unsolicited advice on who you are, what is wrong with you, what you need, and how to do it. It couldn't be further from the truth or what anyone in that situation needs to hear. And how sad it is that so many don't survive because of their own self-loathing and the opinions of others overpower any good sense that they might have left. I have seen the ugly come out of people that I once looked up to or whose opinions mattered to me. Now I saw their horns appear from behind their facades. A good lesson for us all. Ask yourselves this. What makes you think you're a good person? Why do you think the way that you do? And do you walk the talk? Are you making choices that are aligned with who you say you are? Do you make choices that you want or what you think someone wants? We can't read people's minds, so how can we make healthy choices by presumption? I say this because I have seen it. No wonder we have so many questioning their own sanity. People make assumptions based on their own unhealed experiences (that they may or may not be aware of). There is no getting around being a product of your environment, especially when you're stuck in it. I saw it with my own eyes and felt it in my heart. I could finally see when I stopped trying to figure out what I could never understand. I could see that each individual was reacting from their own understanding of things. From their own experience or the lack thereof. The things that were being said to me had nothing to do with the here and now, it had nothing to do with what was going on with me. I was the one who had been asking for help, but no one could hear me. And even though I had asked for help and said

I was taking too much medication; I was not heard. When I say not heard I mean I was given advice to do things that I had already tried and that's what the problem was. I needed to be heard that it was outside of what any of us had an answer to. But I still needed help. It was as if no one could get past "what they know." If they gave me an answer and I still had the problem, then I was the problem. That is a horrible place to be. Because I did feel that way, I started to beat myself up verbally just about every day so that I could get up. I had kind of lost interest in going to doctors and looking to find out what was wrong with me because it had become painfully obvious that there was nothing wrong with me other than ME.

I couldn't stand that the reason for so much chaos in my family and the home we lived in was directly because of me. And that just made me try harder and harder and just made things worse. I was heavy with the weight of dark despair and sadness and trying to fake that I was OK. You get to a point where all the things you were doing to help yourself turn in the other direction without you even having any awareness until it's too late. You're in the pit, and there is no way out. Did you do it on purpose, no. Did you want to ruin your life completely and hurt everyone in it, no. Then why was that the question from so many? No one could see my pain or heartache to make any kind of sense of my terrible behavior. It was just all bad, ugly, and selfish.

I can't remember why other than having really bad stomach pains, the ones that I always was getting. My dad had called to let the outpatient program know that I would have to leave because I was in the hospital. I have two different discharge paperwork that show one of my prescribing doctors whom my dad had kept in contact with. It stated that when I was in the hospital, my dad had made him aware and that I was welcome to come anytime I was able and ready to return. The other forms from the admin say I just stopped showing up, so I was discharged and would not be allowed back into the program. That right there is just one of the reasons that people don't get the help they need. And I have many more to share, so you can see for yourself why it's not as easy as many may think. Just because there is a doctor, a therapist, a hospital, or any other kind of facility where you go for help, it does not mean you're going to get it. Just because a doctor gives you medication, it doesn't mean it's going to be what you need. This is also why it was so hard to get any kind of help when I was trying to do it on my own. You need the help of many if you're going to get back on your feet. You need help, not judgment or the opinions of those wanting to know why you haven't got your shit together.

During this hospital stay, they had to do a liver biopsy. That was one of the most painful procedures I had ever gone through. I didn't think it would be that bad because they just told me to lift my arm, hold still, rubbed with what I was hoping to be something to numb whatever they were getting ready to do on my right side where I was holding my arm over my head. Then they stuck what looked like a hollow needle and put it in and out a couple of times until they were done. As soon as they said OK, you can relax, I crumbled into the fetal position. I was sitting up telling my parents with a smile on my face that it was going to be OK and when they wheeled me out I couldn't speak or move. While I was in the hospital this time, a GI doctor was there, and he was the one who was watching me and doing the tests. I believe I had seen him before outside of there. Somewhere along the line, I had demanded that I see a GI specialist.

I know I saw him after I was discharged. While I was there, he had taken me off the medications they had put me on in the psych hospital, or maybe it was the outpatient program. In the paperwork it showed that there was a direct correlation between the medications, taking on fluids, jaundice, and pain. All of that subsided once I was taken off the medication. Until the next time.

While I was in the hospital, I woke up to the face of someone that I had met in the psych hospital. He, like some of the other people I had met along the way, wanted to help me, save me, I don't know. I was definitely not making any good decisions at that time, whatsoever. But weirdly, sometimes dysfunctional and a bit scary at times, he did help me.

I had gotten a phone call from my husband, and I told him who was visiting, and he was not happy at all. I think he called to say that he and the girls were on the way because they were there not long after he had called. I was so happy to see them. The girls came running in and over to me. My husband introduced himself to my friend, who was visiting, just to be polite. I don't think they were there very long at all because my husband was pissed. Before he left with the girls, he angrily said, "I don't trust him", and then turned around and left me there alone with him.

At that time and probably for about three or four years later I had no idea of time. Time didn't really exist the way it had before. I'm not sure how to explain it. Things would just happen. I would be in the middle of something, somewhere, and not sure how I got there or what happened right before or after, for that matter. My memory was shot. I couldn't remember things that I knew I should have known. I do remember an instance where I got a phone call or a text from my husband, he told me if I wanted to see the girl, I would have to meet him at his game. I had been to the park countless times, so no problem. When it came time to go, I could not remember for the life of me how to get there. I don't know where I went or where I was, but I remember that I had to get somebody to print out directions for me. I remember this story because the printout was in the piles of paperwork, I had saved throughout the years to help me remember things. I don't think I really knew how important saving all this stuff would be until now. And I always got made fun of for dragging a big ol' bag of paperwork around with me everywhere I went. Going through my journals, notes, medical paperwork, etc. really helped me in my healing process. I could put things together and understand a bit of what was going on in my head and what had happened. I had been told and had heard so many different things from different people and I really had to make sense of it myself. It keeps you sick when you listen to other people tell you, "What's wrong with you."

When my husband and the girls left after the visit to the hospital, he called me and told me again that he didn't trust my friend. I always wondered why he left me there with him then.

I think I was in the hospital for about a week. My mom was visiting from Germany at the time to help me and to help out with the girls. When it was time to get discharged from the hospital my mom picked me up. I don't know if he was still with me or if we picked him up, but she dropped us both off at his house. I guess I wasn't allowed to come home. I don't know, and I never really found out. Basically, everything I said and thought was a lie, so I just left it and stopped answering questions, even the ones that I knew I was right and telling the truth. So, I stayed with my friend whom I met at the psych hospital. When I think about it now, I don't know what to think. I guess that was just the way it had to be. I didn't really know how to take care of myself, and I really didn't understand what anybody wanted or expected from me. I'd sleep and not eat. At least here I was getting taken care of. Every once in a while I'd feel a kick against the bed, and I would get handed a yogurt. I will say, he was very thoughtful by always thinking about my stomach and how sick I had been. Why did it take someone I met in a mental hospital to hear and believe how sick I was? He was at the hospital when I had the liver biopsy. He was there but my husband wasn't. Everything at that time didn't make sense and was so outside any kind of normal that it was normal.

While I stayed at his house, he helped me with follow-up doctor appointments, helped me prepare for a colonoscopy, and got me to my appointment. I told him what time to come get me, but it ended up taking hours longer than originally said. When I got into recovery I'd wake up, open my eyes, and back out I went. Over and over, I'd hear my name, look up, and back out. I had woken up in the middle of it, so they had to give me more sedation. So, I'm not sure how long this lasts, being told to wake up and then going right back to sleep. By the time I was awake enough they took me to another room. I was in so much pain, my stomach hurt so bad. They told me it was just air or gas. Whatever it was, my stomach hurt so badly that I was in a cold sweat. They had me lay back down with a cold rag on my forehead and wrapped me in blankets. The nurses who were helping me were trying to ask questions about who was picking me up. No way could I be driving. They told me someone had been there to pick me up hours ago but was not allowed to come back into the recovery area because he was not family. I'm guessing he was there when they kept trying to wake me. So, I had them call my dad. He had no idea what I was doing or where I was in my life at that time. I don't even really know at times. I just existed, sometimes sleeping in my car, sleeping where I could, or at this time I was staying with the guy I met in the mental hospital. My dad came to pick me up, and there I was rolled up in blankets with a rag on my head and complaining of the pain. I couldn't stand up straight. He helped me to his car, and I told him to drive to my friend's place. I didn't know where else to go. I wasn't allowed to come home. When we got there, the wrought iron gate that went around the house was locked, and my car wasn't there. I don't know where it was or where he had gone. I told my dad it was OK, he could just drop me I'm sure he would be there at any time. I was trying to be as "normal" as I possibly could. I was in so much pain, I just needed to lay down and I could barely stand. I just wanted him to go and not worry. Whenever I had my moments of clarity and realized all the pain and confusion I had created, it made me want to use again. I was so so sad. My dad drove off and when I saw that he was far enough I went across the street and asked the neighbor for a ladder and to come help me get over the gate. I went up and over, and he took the ladder back. I went to the side of the house. Not too far off from under the kitchen window was a water spigot. I pushed the window all the way open, put my foot on the water spigot, and pushed myself up. I had no energy at all and I landed on my stomach and blacked out. It wasn't for long. I just kind of came to with everything spinning and blurry. I crawled across the counter knocking over glasses and other dirty dishes that were on the side of the sink. I left everything as it was and went straight to the bed that I could see through the open bedroom door. And there I would lay down just trying to catch my breath. I barely had enough energy to even breathe. I didn't have anything left.

I was in and out for days. I got a couple of phone calls, getting yelled at for "shacking up with someone else." I just wanted to sleep. "Shacking up," where was I supposed to go? I'm not allowed to go home, but I'm being yelled at for staying there. The next time I got up, I was to go to a follow-up to see my GI specialist. I kept all the paperwork my doctors gave me, so I could go back to make sense of it later if I couldn't then. Trying to take care of myself was impossible. The notes from my GI said that we had agreed that my body had been through enough and that I should take a break from trying to figure out what medications I could take. In retrospect, that is a decision that should be made by all doctors involved, not just one. That was one of the biggest problems I ran into when I was trying to let all doctors know what a different doctor did or gave me to take. If I wasn't directly asked a question, I didn't share. It wasn't that I was trying to hide anything. I was disabled in every sense of the word but didn't have the words or any real insight into what that really meant. I was mentally, physically, emotionally, and spiritually disabled. How on earth did anyone expect me to do any of this? It blows me away when I think about it. The more unable I was to do things, the more I would get yelled at. Or I would get comments that made my already questioning mind implode on itself. Why would anyone think that I would behave like this on purpose? A healthy person doesn't just stop knowing how to take care of themselves. I mean, I just don't get it.

CHAPTER SEVEN

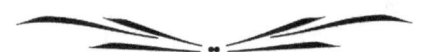

I had been given separation papers three days after coming out of the mental institution. I knew I was on my own. On my own, being half the person that I used to be, if even that. I'm dealing with my physical health, my mental health, my emotional health, and my spiritual health and I'm having a hard time remembering things. The more I get barked at, the more I want to run for my life.

I can't take being told what to do. That doesn't mean I was trying to be difficult, even though that's what I was being told. I was constantly being asked why I always wanted to argue. I didn't want to argue. I was fighting for my life. Being told what to do when I had already tried whatever was being told to me, or what I knew I did not need. It's maddening, absolutely maddening. You have no voice because of the label you're given, you just don't matter anymore. This is why people snap. You just get pushed into giving up, one way or another. You either give up fighting for your life or you give in to the labels. You get beat down into accepting a fate that isn't yours to accept.

I found an apartment that was within walking distance of the outpatient drug recovery program, which I went to. Acupuncturist, which I went to, and the hospital where I also had been to before and went to again. I know now that the worst thing I did and what made it so hard was trying to get clean with someone who needed their own help. Great intentions but not realistic. But I also didn't have any other options. And nothing is realistic. Mental illness and addiction are illnesses that are thought to be "a you problem," so you have to figure out how to get the help that you need. At that time, even though I was somewhat functioning, I wasn't on any medication nor was I doing anything for my mental health or really my physical either. I still thought that it was a "me" problem, and the "me" problem was that I was back on drugs. I didn't know how to function. Still dealing with my stomach and my mental health and now trying to get off drugs at a time when my daughters are begging for me and my marriage is falling apart. I didn't say the things I did to my husband because I wanted to hurt him; I said them because I was dying. I needed help.At first, I thought we were on the same page. He was taking care of the kids while I was getting help. But every time he called and told me when I could see the girls, he never asked if I was able. I would most likely use again. I couldn't move or go outside without using. I had been yelled at so many times and told things that just didn't make any sense to me. I found out later from my daughters that they were being told that I had abandoned them. The pain that I was feeling before all of this was unbearable and that's why I ended up telling on myself. That's why I said whatever I needed to say so I could get some help. And now I feel like I'm getting kicked in the face every time I leave the house or answer the phone. I was already holding on to a very thin rope. I used, so I could see the girls. I would use every time I had to go out to do anything now. I told on myself because I needed help in every which way. And now I was a completely different person. I had been a completely different person for about 4 years. Not only did I have to heal mentally, but my memory was also gone, my anxiety made me physically ill, and no one wanted to hear it. It's just a never-ending cycle of complete defeat. For years I tried making sense of what had happened mixed with the actions and what people said to me. It made it even worse. No one asked what happened and how could they help. I was told to stop living in the past if I tried talking about anything that had happened. I wasn't living in the past, that was the place I was living in in my mind and could not get out. I might as well as be told, "I'm not listening, and I could give a shit because you are really inconveniencing me and my life. Now go and get your shit together." It took me a few years to stop thinking about why and work hard at letting go. Yes, as weird as that sounds to work hard at letting go. I was terrified. But as soon as I let go of trying to figure things out the way that I understood them, the more I started to understand. It's called surrender. And that was another thing that I didn't understand for the longest time. I didn't think I could surrender until I had everything figured out. And that is the opposite of surrender. I tried so hard and that was the part that was killing me. I was holding on to what I thought I knew and what I thought was best. But if you are truly going to heal you have to let go because that is the very thing that will kill you if you don't. Surrender was to give it up. But it is to give up on everything you think you know and give it to God. One of the hardest things I have ever had to do. He gave me a chance before and look where I am now. I didn't think he would want anything to do with me, let alone catch me when I jumped. An unexplainable beauty. The Devil was in my ear the whole way, laughing at me, telling me I was worthless and a joke for thinking God would be there for a piece of shit like me. I wanted to give up so many times, but the thought of that was even more painful. Torture beyond comprehension until one day it was all gone. Once I put all my faith into God, the universe, infinite love, and light, I never turned back. No matter what hardships came up, I could handle every single one because I had definitely been through worse and now had faith and an understanding of what I was capable of. I had a knowing without knowing, and I was never going to let go of that ever. The Devil still tried to take me down, trust me and this was the battle of the battles. But honestly, I am the strongest person I know, so I'm not backing down anytime soon. In fact, after all of this that has happened, no way. You can't take me out. I won't let you. And what makes me even stronger is the fact that God made me this way. When I feel weak, I remind myself of who God made me to be and then remind myself that I can do anything with him by my side.

I got tired of being sick and not trusting my own mind. It was all too much. I went to acupuncture because I had done all the traditional ways before, so now, I was going to do whatever I could think of. It was the acupuncture place that was within walking distance from the apartment that I was renting. I used money from a credit line that my husband and I had. On my second appointment with the acupuncturist, I had the same person that I had before. She was really nice and we got along great so I thought I could share with her what I was doing and why. In short, when I said I was trying to get off heroin she morphed into another person. I saw an ugly come out of her that was beyond disgusting. She was disgusted with me. She looked at me like I was a worthless human being. Forget the reason for how I got there. Her demeanor didn't change when I said I was first addicted to the pain pills my doctor was giving me. It was OK to be addicted to pills that your doctor gave you, but you're a worthless piece of shit when you're doing heroin. They are all the same thing, by the way, just a different way of using them.

She finished putting the needles in very aggressively, walked out, and shut the door. As if I didn't already have a fear of just about anything and everyone. I opened up to her in hopes of some direction or sympathy, **anything**. When it came down to it, I felt like a baby and needed somebody to feel sorry for me and take care of me. I wanted to feel like I mattered. I see again how humans work. They can't see the good in the bad; they just focus on the bad. Yes, it was a terrible thing because I didn't want to be in this situation either, and I was trying to get help. But then again, I am a human being. I still can't understand how anyone can treat another human being like this. I really had seen and done so much in this world but at the same time was so naïve to human behavior. I thought I was the bad guy, I wouldn't treat anyone like this.

Around the corner from the apartment and down the street from the acupuncture place was a drug recovery program that I was in. One of the hardest things to do for an addict is to allow themselves to get sick or be unwell. To be in one of these programs you have to stop using long enough until your body starts to go into withdrawal. If you were asked to do this before addiction, I mean real addiction, this would be no problem. You could still make sense of what you were getting ready to do and why. Addiction completely robs you of yourself and any rational thought processes you might have possessed before. You are completely drained of yourself. You have no problem-solving skills and everything is too much to bear or comprehend.

I made the longest walk ever, getting to my appointment to start the program. I hadn't used, so I could start taking Suboxone. I had done this so many times before, and it never got any easier. In fact, the thought of being dope sick is a power the Devil holds over you that you have to fight every second after every second. Put your guard down and you'll have yourself talked out of doing this and back home using before you even realize that you left the place. Drugs are the devil. I take that back. Addiction is the devil. Doing drugs—good, bad, right, or wrong—is a choice that you can make. Addiction is the devil, simple as that. And don't think that prescription medications aren't the same because they are, you get just as sick when your body has become habituated. Habituated would be a nice way of saying addicted. Maybe that's what that drug dealer heard when I was whining about what was going on. I told him my whole sob story and that I didn't know what to do anymore. What he heard was that I was dope sick. I've had this argument with so many people who refuse to believe that these are one and the same. One is synthetic and the other one isn't, that's it. That of course was the argument I would never win. But I am telling you now; and yes, I will argue my point. And don't think that people didn't inject doctor-prescribed pain pills. And some of those were way worse than heroin. Again, I said to those that didn't care, didn't want to listen, **didn't want to** hear it, or thought I was full of shit just like everything else that came out of my mouth. I was an untrustworthy liar. Or too stupid to matter because I was on drugs.

I already wasn't feeling good and holding on for dear life trying to make it until I could take the Suboxone. I answered a bunch of agonizing repetitive questions for what seemed like hours. After taking the first dose they watched to see if you needed more or how your body was adjusting. After about 20 minutes, which feels way longer, I get another dose because I feel worse than I did before. They think it's because I don't have a high enough dose, but I know it's something else, but nobody listens. The next thing I know I'm in my counselor's office on the floor rolled up in a ball. My stomach hurts so badly, I'm rocking back and forth in cold sweats. The nurse or whoever the person was, said after a blood test that there was methadone in my system and asked me why I took that if I was coming here. I told her I didn't and that I hadn't taken any methadone, ever. However, you cannot argue with anyone about anything when you are in the position that you are in. I question how anyone ever makes it through this stuff. Actually, I have a great understanding of why they don't. When I finally just said OK, she said it could have been in the heroin I was using. I had never heard that before. She gave me a whole rundown on people putting methadone in the heroin because it was cheaper or something. I didn't get anything she was trying to explain, I didn't understand, and honestly, I just wanted to get out of there, so I could go home so that I could use. Addiction just drains you of everything. You can't handle being sick, you can't handle anything. I left there, went home, and made a phone call. It didn't really help me, it just made it so I wasn't rolled up in a ball. Don't ask me. I never understood any of it. I used and I didn't use. I felt a certain way and would tell whoever was asking what I used and when. More so than not they told me when and what I used and why. I don't know why I even bothered at times. It is so hard not to give up. Everyone has an opinion about you and who you are when you're on drugs. Even when you're asking for help, you're treated like a criminal. These are some of the exact reasons why others don't make it. They just give up. You either continue the lifestyle or if you do try getting clean that whole process could kill you if you don't make it to the other side. You just start losing sense and hope and have beaten yourself up verbally to the point of seeing yourself as worthless as the people around you are treating you. It is an ugly, sad, and pathetic existence. I wouldn't wish it on anyone.

Even though I had the three places I had within walking distance of my apartment, I made the worst decision believing that someone who was in the same position as me could help me in my position. It was the blind leading the blind. The environment was the worst place I could have been. It was way too easy to get drugs with the people that came in and out of there. My story was slowly changing, and the conversations were about my relationship with my husband and where he was. He doesn't give a shit about you is all I heard, and I believed it. I had so much coming at me from all angles I really didn't know who to believe in anymore. Everything and everyone was too much for me. I started using more and less trying to take care of myself. I was giving up. What I thought was the bottom, where things could not get any worse got worse. Too much for me to wrap my head around. I was already holding on by a thread and every negative word said to me was like someone holding my head underwater. Even more afraid than I was before. I stayed in that apartment for about a year and thought things would get better. I stayed with a friend but we were both using. I can't really tell you much about that time. What I was doing with myself? I had the right intentions but so unaware of how and what to do. And I didn't know until years later how bad my memory had gotten. So many times I had dreams of my husband kicking the front door into the apartment to come get me and take me home. I kept waiting for him to not be so mad at me, for him to realize that I needed help. This wasn't me. I don't know. I think my husband and family gave up on me. The first Christmas and my birthday in January drained even more of the will to live. On my birthday I got no calls, nothing. I lay on the living room floor crying for hours. I was freezing cold by the time my roommate came home, saw me on the floor, got me up, and put me to bed. I thought I would die of a broken heart. Eventually, all of the people that you've been trying to get away from are your only and closest friends. They were the only ones who listened and understood me. But they were all as sick as I was but with their own reasons. So many sad and disturbing conversations. So many sad and disturbing actions.

I heard some yelling and went to the hallway; someone that I didn't know was there walking around in circles yelling. I looked to the bathroom and saw someone lying on the floor, and the guy in the background yelling that he od'd. I rolled him on his back and started mouth-to-mouth and compressions. And that wouldn't be the first time. Terrifying, the seconds and minutes tick by until a gasp for air at last.

CHAPTER EIGHT

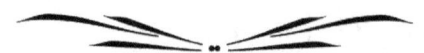

I had to get out, out to where, I don't know. I was so far gone and removed that I didn't think I would ever have the life that I was trying so hard to get back to. At the same time, I started losing the ability to see past right where I was. It was a joke to think that I would ever get out. Here I was again, sucked in with no way out. I had lived in the apartment for about a year, I think. I was using a credit line that my husband and I had, well, I guess it was just his by this time. I had tried so many times to get some kind of financial help and was turned down every time. Most would look at me like I was, well, like I was crazy. I was married and at that time I was still wearing my wedding ring, which was not a small one, so why did I need the help? But I didn't know what to do. I don't know if I mentioned it before, but my things had started to get packed up by my mother-in-law when I first went into the mental institution. I was terrified of everything and everyone. I didn't know where to go or who to ask for help from. This was a road where doing by yourself was impossible. I needed stability more than anything, and I was living by a second-to-second existence.

My panic attacks were so bad at times that I couldn't leave the house. I couldn't move. My mom had told me that she had come by to see me when she was here to help with the girls. I made her wait for two hours in the car before I came out. I didn't mean to do those things. I also didn't know it then but I had PTSD. I couldn't get myself to leave the house without verbally abusing myself. Shacking in fear and telling myself to get my shit together. Questioning myself on how I could be afraid of my own mother. But it wasn't her in particular. I was irrationally afraid of everything.

My first priority in all of this from the beginning was to get clean. I was an embarrassment and like I had been told, "barely a babysitter." I fought my own thoughts constantly. Should I give up because the girls did not deserve to have me as a mother? I had hurt them enough. Those thoughts with the devil laughing in my ear about what a piece of shit, worthless human being I was, was beyond torture. And whenever I got and went just a little bit in the right direction, I'd get barked at. I would be told if I wanted to see the girls it was...now or nothing. But I wasn't ready. And being yelled at would make me go right back to using. All the work I had done would just be a waste of time. I did the work but nobody else did. I still got treated the same way. I got treated like a piece of garbage. All of my work was gone because I could not, "be normal." I had to use in order to see my children. It hurt way too badly and I could not face that kind of pain anymore. I was dying of a broken heart, a slow agonizing torturous death. What I was fighting for was killing me at the same time. Stuck in the pit of hopelessness, sadness, and pain. The ugly slow demise that you have created for yourself. That's what you get for being you.

After the apartment, I lived in a couple of different places, including couches, garages, and my car. I try here and there to do outpatient programs but I forget to go to the appointments or I don't have money to get gas to get to the appointment. I just don't know how to take care of myself more than just the basics. The last place I stayed was at an old friend of mine. I had known him since junior high but lost contact after our twenties. When we moved back from San Francisco to Sacramento, my husband was adamant that I connect with old friends. In retrospect, maybe he did see and understand my depression. I had found and connected with a few but I didn't want to reach out in the first place. Everyone was doing drugs or drinking. It seems like everybody is on something. Or partying like rock stars when they have the night off from the kids. Imagine that, going to a parent's house that we have befriended who has a big bag of Vicodin. I couldn't get away from it. People that my husband worked with that he would have never even thought would be doing drugs were doing drugs and offering them to me. In their eyes it wasn't that big of a deal, they weren't, "real drugs", they were doctor-prescribed. HA, it's all the same thing, people. I won't go off on a tangent on synthetic heroin in a pill, but please hear me when I say pharmaceuticals are and can be 10 times worse than whatever you're buying off the streets.

So, I'm not sure how we connected again but he let me sleep on his couch. I kept trying to "plan" what I had to do to help myself with it only to fall through just as fast as I had written it down to do it. I was planning to plan, but I was getting nowhere. I tried seeing my children, but the first time I saw my family, my girls walked away with another woman, well I really didn't care anymore. I didn't care about myself, in fact, I hated myself. I had tried to "fix me," and I failed. I had failed and let everyone down. I just couldn't make sense of anything anymore.

Somehow I still had a piece of paper that my mom and her friend had given me with a number on it about a dual diagnosis recovery center. I didn't even know what dual diagnosis was and that would be exactly the place that I needed to go. I called the number. The person on the other line asked me questions, which I kept trying to weasel out of. I still thought I knew what I needed and had it all figured out. Thank God this guy was well-trained and had probably heard all the excuses or "big plans" before. He asked me if I could get someone to fly me out to Southern California for treatment. No way. I wasn't going to ask anyone to spend money on me. I was a waste of space. After a few more minutes of conversation with him, I said, "Maybe my stepbrother." He flies a lot, so maybe he has some reward points. And that's all that it took. He just kept fishing to get a phone number. Two days later, if even that, my stepbrother was picking me up and taking me to the airport. He saved my life. But it wasn't going to be easy. I had to start all over again and here we go again. And I mean, here we go again.

I start the journey at a house with 8–10 girls, not sure. We have a house manager and staff. Staff means more than likely someone with lived experience, maybe going to school or finishing school studying mental illness or addiction. The first week is about getting settled in, seeing a psychiatrist, arranging medications, and detoxing. The first few days were fine. I had started on medications, not sure which ones, but bipolar was still a part of the story, so it was either mood stabilizers, antipsychotics, or both. I had also been on medication for detox. I had started having some stomach pains but not too bad. A day or two later, I'm lying in my bed curled up in a ball rocking back and forth in a cold sweat. One of the other girls saw me and went to get me some help. She came back and told me that the house manager said I would be fine; it was just part of detox. I argued that it was not detox. I know detox, I know withdrawal, and I know my stomach issues. And I know when I am in a lot of pain. Nothing. It took some time for the girls in the house to convince the staff to do something and to check on me. She came in and took my temperature, and I was burning up, so finally off to emergency we went. Just like so many other places and people before this, when you say "drug" in any way, it changes the way people see you and treat you. The staff that was with me explained that I had just started treatment and that I had been experiencing stomach pains after only a few days of being there. He pressed around on my stomach, did a female exam, and said it was probably a sexually transmitted infection, so he gave me a prescription for antibiotics and said they would call if anything else came up from the exam. I was in too much pain to say anything. How can I have sexually transmitted anything if I haven't had or been having sex? We went back to the house, started the antibiotics, and I was still lying in bed rocking. Another day or two go by. I ended up having to go back to the hospital because I felt worse than I did before.

They were short-staffed, so nobody could take me. It took all the girls in the house to advocate for me to have them call an ambulance. The ambulance took me to the hospital but didn't have a place to put me. They had me wait in a chair because they took back the gurney I was on. I really needed someone there with me. I was in so much pain I could barely talk. I'm freezing and having a hard time sitting up. I'm sliding around in a chair trying to get some kind of comfortable and warm up. They finally came out, put me in a wheelchair, and brought me to the back. I hadn't been back there very long until I was leaning over the side throwing up what looked like brown tar or sludge. I had thrown up a couple of times and then they moved me to another area. A few minutes later, Elizabeth, one of the girls in the program, showed up. She came in to help and check on me. A person I had known for about a week was there for me when I was so sick and alone. She was in the room when a nurse came by asking me to sign do not resuscitate papers. I didn't really know what I was signing, and Elizabeth told me to stop. She said, "No way you are signing anything, and I want your dad's phone number." I need to understand what's going on here. She called him, but I don't really know what they discussed. But she could understand a bit better now that I had been dealing with stomach issues for a while now. They transferred me to another room where I would stay for about a week. It was interesting to see the difference between how I was treated when I was just a drug addict and when they found out I had insurance. It was like night and day. When I had been admitted and didn't have the staff from the facility, saying over and over that was in recovery, I was treated like a human again. The labels will be the difference between life and death. The labels will be the difference between whether you matter or don't.

I'm at a great big hospital in Southern California now. Too bad I wasn't able to advocate for myself at that time. And after I had been admitted, Elizabeth wasn't allowed to come in. I wasn't able to get it across that I had been dealing with stomach issues, amongst other things for years. And this time the diagnosis was pancreatitis. I was throwing up, what looked like motor oil. Like dark green sludge.

I am so thankful for the recovery place I was at. Even with, let's call them mishaps, they did their best and helped me tremendously. They had to discharge me from the program while I was in the hospital and then reinstate me when I came back. And they would be the ones that would pick me back up from the hospital. I had been given discharge papers with follow-up directions: one would be to come back and see a doctor there and another was to set up an appointment with a GI specialist. That appointment couldn't happen then, and I was told to do that whenever I got back home. I'm guessing because I was in a recovery program, I wasn't to be driven around to doctor's appointments. I get it. By the time I got out of treatment and got back home, I had to start all over again. That's another story.

Now that I'm back in the program I hit the ground running. Even though I still have the bipolar diagnosis following me and the medications that go with it, I'm in a better place. I'm in a better place in the sense that I know I'm going to get the help I need and can't do it myself. I'm in a dual diagnosis facility working on my mental health and my addiction at the same time. And once I had the initial hospitalizations behind me, I only had the two to worry about. Meaning I could focus on my mental health and recovery. It was like night and day. When you're working on yourself with others who are going through the same, well, it's what you need. I needed to be in an environment that was nothing but recovery, not just getting through it. I'm not saying it was easy or that that was all I needed. I still had a long hard road in front of me. But I had to get some kind of stable first. I was there for around 9–10 months and had lived a completely other lifetime.

After a few months in, I went home to see my girls. Both times were a bust. I was still in no way ready to see them; it hurt me so bad. To see my sweet baby girls, calling out, "Mama, mommy, is that really you?" I died an agonizing death a thousand times, I couldn't take it. My guilt, sadness, and shame were too much for me to handle. I had seen them and then was supposed to see them the following day, I believe. I drank instead. I went back to the program with my head hung low with disappointment and understanding that I had to start all over again. The more work you do, the better you do, and the more advancement you get. I would have transferred to sober living, but I blew it. I'm not and haven't been OK with my medication though either. One day in group the director of the program calls me out of class. Yes, we have classes to learn how the addicted brain works amongst other things. Anyway, I go into his office and he tells me that I'm scaring people and that they will be transferring me to a mental institution to tweak my medications. I lost it. I was sobbing. First, I was heartbroken that I was scaring people that badly, and I needed to be sent away. And second, I was terrified that I was going to be left and forgotten. I begged them not to forget me. I begged him to please not forget that I was there. He had another one of their therapists that I got along with really well come in. I knew and could feel his sincerity when he said he thought so highly of me and wanted nothing but the best for me. He assured me that this was just to get medications in check and that he looked forward to me coming back to pick up right where we left off.

They had one of the other staff that helps out with transportation take me to a place in San Bernardino. We sat in the intake office for a while and I was fine. The conversation was fine until it wasn't. I have no idea what was said or why but I basically got up in her face, mad and having no idea what I was saying to her. I liked her, and she liked me. I don't know what that was, but I will say as I have before: that those medications are no joke. If you're not psychotic, they'll make you psychotic. I would apologize profusely when I got back to the program.

I was there for a few weeks. What a roller-coaster ride that was. The weaning from the medications, the changing of the medications, and the combinations of medications. WOW!! I paced the hallway in front of my room day and night, up and down. I thought I heard voices coming through the pipes and the drains. Everything was really intense. I was in another world. And not one that I liked being in. When I first got there, I had to go through "the process." This very scary, horrid actually, unkempt beast of a woman coming up to me and telling me I have to go to another room. I go in and thank God I wasn't left alone with her when another nurse came in. The women told me I had to take all of my clothes off to see what sex I was. I told her I was female, but you don't have a say in these places. I cried and took my clothes off and on as fast as I could. It was bullshit. This time I would stay in one room with a roommate my whole stay. I don't know how I got released from this place when I did because I still was not OK. But I was no longer outwardly not ok. When I got back I was told I had been moved to a different house. I had moved houses on several different occasions. I guess it was every time I had to leave and come back I would have to start over somewhere different.

So, while I'm there I'm doing great. I'm one of their best students. I am doing everything that I possibly can to get what I need to "fix me." Throughout my stay, a huge trigger that would send me into a downward spiral every time was the divorce papers. My now ex-husband had sent divorce papers to the first facility. When I would be told about them, it just made me sick every time. I could not wrap my head around trying to figure out a divorce right now. And what about my children? I didn't understand that I didn't understand yet once again. I tried hiding from them. I couldn't take the papers. I didn't know how to. It might sound funny that I didn't know how to, but I didn't. My mind was incapable of making any kind of sense of what that all entailed. Yes, he had a girlfriend he was now living with, but that still didn't help me understand. What did that mean for me and my children? I was terrified to sign those papers. I was horrified of even holding that envelope. It would follow me from one treatment house to another, I couldn't get away. I was working on trying to understand my illness, what addiction is, and what medications work for me. I couldn't sign those papers.

I went home again a few months later. I should have known better from the last time that I wasn't ready. But I didn't really realize that I wasn't ready at the time. I only know that now. It would take me a while, years, in fact, to get stable and healthy. This time I don't know why but it was more intense than the time before. I can't begin to tell you what kind of pain it is when your children are reaching out and need you and you don't know how to respond. There was still some kind of darkness that was keeping me from getting to them. I had heard in treatment over and over that "just because you have changed, it doesn't mean anyone or anything else has." I understood the words, but I didn't know what that meant. The people, the questions, everything was the same. The go-go-go and being around people with the same questions was something that I had to work on if I was ever going to get healthy. I had to get to a point where I would understand that no one would ever understand or change. I was the one that had to change. I had to understand that most didn't even think about changing because they didn't have to look at themselves. After all, I was the obvious problem and the one who had done all these terrible deeds. I was the one with the problem. Why on earth would anyone have to try to understand anything? It's been taught to us to believe that the person with mental health issues or drug addiction is the only one with the problem.

On this trip after seeing the girls, I used. This time, I would drive my car back, taking about a week to get back, or it feels like it did. I smoked meth and slowly worked my way back to treatment. I couldn't stand the thought of going back, and I couldn't stand the fact that I used to. I had come so far and I totally self-sabotaged myself. I don't even like meth, it makes me feel worse. I would make it back, ashamed of myself, and I would have to start all over again. I don't know how long I've been back, not long, and I'm lying in bed facing the wall. I just lay there rocking and begging God to have mercy. I was under serious attack. I did not do myself any favors for using the devil's drug again, and I was getting ready to lose it. In the background I can hear one of the staff, "Is Jessica back, the divorce papers got sent to her." It was like nails on a chalkboard. I can't take it, those divorce papers again. Being told about those divorce papers again, I just couldn't take it. I did not have the mental capacity. I was told to get up time and time again, and I just kept rocking. I couldn't turn around to the chaos of the other girls running around, doing I don't know what, but it was too much for me. Staff kept yelling at me and I finally got someone's attention that I needed to see my case manager. She comes over, "Come on, Jessica, we have to get up…" "Please listen to me," I begged her. "I have to go somewhere else, something is going to happen if I stay here. I'm not in the right place. Please get me out of here." I rocked and begged God for mercy. She asked me questions and I guess they were what she needed to hear to understand that I needed to go to a psychiatric hospital, and I needed to go now. I just lay there and prayed until someone finally came and said we were just waiting for transportation. Someone would be right there and we left. I went to a different place than last time, I can't remember where this place was.

I had to go through the intake again but it gave me a sense of relief because I was in the right place. I knew I needed to be there. I saw a therapist and was put back on medication, and I participated in the groups within a couple of days. But I stayed in bed for the first couple of days. I stayed there for a few weeks with no mishaps and was ready to go back to treatment. So once again my treatment facility that I was at discharged me from there and enrolled me back into the program. I would have never, ever, succeeded had I not mysteriously found that number to call to get me into the dual diagnosis treatment. Even though I had some difficulty with the diagnosis and the medications, it was everything else that I needed. I needed to eat, sleep, breathe, and recover. Instead of being in an environment that hurt me, whether from others or myself. When you're in it, it is close to impossible to heal. You need to get away from it all. You have to get away from others telling you what you need to do or when they have expectations that you just can't do. It takes time to heal and a lot of hard work and dedication. Yes, sure you can just quit doing drugs, you can pretend that you're OK when you're not, and you can keep on telling others, "I'm fine" when you're not. You can put it down and push yourself because that's what you have been taught to do, or you can do the work to heal and understand why you got there in the first place. You can learn how your brain works and understand your mental illness. And if you are really going to heal, then you don't use your mental illness as an excuse, but you learn how to navigate it and what you need to do be really be OK. You must find out what you need in mind, body, and spirit to be the best and healthiest version of yourself. Something we should all do, mental illness or not.

After a few weeks in the psychiatric hospital, I was released back into the care of the dual diagnosis treatment center. At some point in that time back, the divorce papers are following me around again. I had gotten a few calls from my now ex telling me to sign them. I'm still struggling to understand. I'm scared. But I couldn't get away from it or his calls. I said I needed help with it, and he said he would send a notary. I didn't know how to stand up for myself at that time, so I had no choice. The notary came and one of the counselors came with me into the room where we were to meet. I was terrified. I kept trying to ask questions but was told by both of them in different ways that they could not give any kind of legal advice. I was on my own, and I just signed where I was told to sign. I tried reading it and couldn't comprehend what any of it meant. After that, I could only focus on how I would finish my recovery, how would I eat, how would I pay for medication, and where would I live after this. I can understand that my now ex-husband wanted to get on with his life, but what am I going to do? I just signed everything away. I didn't totally get it right then and there, but I signed everything away, including my children.

CHAPTER NINE

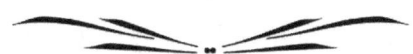

After I signed the paperwork, everything changed. My need and want to get healthy was replaced with a fear and worry of what I was to do next. I still didn't know how to take care of myself, and I had been turned down for temporary disability. And I was scared to death about no longer having health insurance. I was just scared of everything. I was right back in the same situation I was before. The only difference is I have done some healing and some work, but I will be going right back into the same environment. The same environment with the same people that hurt me either directly or indirectly. Again, I hope that these words are read throughout this book to bring some awareness to all of our behavior. How a large majority of us are showing up in this world unless we decide to take a look at ourselves to make a change.

It takes every bit of mental, physical, and emotional strength to get to see the girls. I'm still not understanding what is being said to me or understanding people's behavior. The only way I can see the girls is at their games surrounded by all of the people who yelled at me, turned their backs on me, and basically left me for dead. And I am still a shell of myself. My panic attacks are so bad I feel like I'm going to pass out with just the thought of going to see the girls. Every single fear and emotion comes up, and it takes everything in me to make it out the front door. I sometimes don't even get to see the girls other than from the bleachers. I don't understand why everyone is just OK with this new girlfriend playing mother to my children. It's like I just don't matter anymore. Life goes on and you've been replaced. This whole story that I abandoned my girls and thank God this new person is here to save the girls from me is a lie. This was the rational decision made to help my children, to tell them that I abandoned them and have someone come in to replace me. To play happy family like nothing has happened is the logical solution. This is the best solution that we can come up with after the girls have already been through so much, let's put them through some more.

I had to find a job. I had to find a community. I had to find a doctor. I had to find a therapist. I had to figure out how to live my life and start it over from scratch. So, one after another, I make the appointments. I go to some, I'm getting on my feet, and then I get one canceled appointment after another because I don't have any insurance. The roller coaster ride starts again. I'm not sure exactly how this part went down but the doctor that I was seeing refilled enough for me to wean off some of my medications. But the antipsychotics would be cut off cold turkey and I was a mess. And when I say a mess, I mean I am back to fighting the devil.

So bear with me here. I'm not really sure how this starts or how it goes down. We haven't gone to court and, my ex is telling me what he will do for me. He says that he will give me half the money from the sale of our house and six months of Cobra Health insurance or something, but that would be something I have to figure out. I don't have a clue if he paid for that or what. I was fighting the devil, I didn't have anything extra to try to figure out health insurance. I didn't really agree with being told once again about what I was to accept. He would give me this and he and his new girlfriend would tell me how and when I would see my children. And I would be repeatedly TOLD everything.

I knew I didn't have it in me, yet. I didn't have the strength to fight, yet. And no, it wasn't about fighting with him. It was fighting for myself and my girls. But first I had to get myself together. This roller coaster ride that I was on had me terrified once again. I had even bought charms and religious artifacts to "protect" me because I couldn't sleep. I was afraid to sleep. It was as bad as being on drugs again or trying to get off them. Antipsychotics are not for the faint of heart. Especially because I wasn't supposed to be on them in the first place. And then going cold turkey. I'm just not in a good place, but I was better than before. I am grateful for the understanding that I don't have to have the answers to how I will get myself out of this, I just know that I will. I have all of the faith in the world because I have already been shown. I didn't even know how I had gotten as far as I already had but I wasn't going to give up now, no matter how hard it was. I had made a decision, and my girls were going to get their mother back. I was going to get my girls back and they would get a healthy mom.

I don't have a clue how I did it. I ended up getting on Medi-Cal and started the whole building of my "treatment team." I knew I needed it all. I had to build something like I had at the dual diagnosis treatment place that I had just left. Everything under one roof if you will. Co-accruing or dual diagnosis kind of thing. An MD, therapist, groups, etc. You need a team. You need to work on the whole you, mind, body, and soul. You cannot overcompensate in one area to pretend that the other areas don't exist. You can't drink it, drug it, sex it, work it, or anything else it away. You just have to go head-on with the whole of you. And yes, I get how scary that is, but only because we've been taught a bunch of backward crap. We've been taught to fear but not to question the fear or where it comes from. Or we've been taught that we know better and have the answers to everything, so we don't allow ourselves the opportunity to learn something new.

This is where this gets good. I started putting it all together in getting started with an outpatient program. I'm terrified of not having everything in place. I don't yet trust myself because I don't even know how to function correctly. I don't trust anyone. I'm just not there yet. I met one person at a time, different positions but all were a part of this program. Then I meet Stephanie. Stephine Wicks NP. Now, I have to really drive this home and explain my fear and distrust of people at this time. I had explained or tried to explain myself so many times before, but that bipolar label I could not shake. I am still very aware of how hard it is for people to listen to someone say, I'm not bipolar, even though you're on medication for it and your records from the last several years say otherwise. I just need someone to look at me, to take their eyes off the screen or their charts and paperwork, and to look at me and hear me. Just to take the time in hearing me out, and I don't give a shit what it looks like, hear me out.

I opened up slowly. Testing the waters. Was she really hearing me? Was she listening and understanding what I was sharing with her? I've been fighting for my life for years, and I was the only one besides God who actually knew how true that statement was. Her words after our conversation were something along the lines of "...we aren't going to diagnose just yet, and we aren't going to ever put you on antipsychotics, and we will start you with one medication at a time starting with your thyroid." It brings me to tears as I write and reread these words. And we did that one medication at a time, one antidepressant at a time, and I never ever took another mood stabilizer or antipsychotic again. She saved my life.

I knew I was going to be OK. I knew I was going to get on my feet. I knew I was going to get my girls back. Once I was a little more stable I started taking a psychology class. I started looking for a job and one that had to do with mental health and/or addiction. I wanted and needed to be involved in every way possible. I was on a mission and this was the beginning of it all. I was never going to be in a position, ever again, where other people had more control over me than I did myself. Would everything just fall into place, as I had envisioned, nope, not just yet. But I have made a commitment, I have come so far. I'm not stopping. Nothing is going to stop me. I've been shown too much to stop. Meaning, that the more I move forward, the more that is revealed to me, the more I see people for who they really are.

CHAPTER TEN

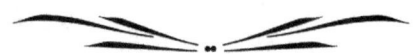

I started researching attorneys and what a nightmare that was. I was an absolute wreck. And I was not doing myself any favors at all. I could barely talk about any of what had happened, and I needed to share it all and be honest or I wouldn't get the representation that I needed. I felt so small and judged. It sucked the life out of me every time. I only went to a couple and then decided on one. Or should I say I found one that would take me? I have such mixed emotions about that whole experience. I was always in the back of my mind wondering if he was really going to help me or not. I don't know if it was my own paranoia or if I was really reading him. You know I'm still not anywhere near OK or grounded. I don't even really know how bad it still is, it's me looking back at that time now and being able to really see it. I was on a mission though. And I did not know how long the process was going to take, so I had to start now. I had to start the process and then meet up with where I needed to be as a mother when the time came. I could not wait until I was 100%, I did not really know if that day would ever come, so I had to act now before any more time had passed.

It was so embarrassing, belittling, shameful, and every other kind of horribly uncomfortable. The questions I was being asked were torture. Of course, I can understand why I'm being asked these questions, I get it. But that didn't make it any easier. I am well aware that I was doing drugs and that I was in a mental institution, so I am going to be under some pressure. It doesn't matter how or why I got to where I did, I get it. It's devastating and I am the cause. But I still hadn't gotten the help, meaning the therapy that I would eventually get and so badly needed, so this was like razor blades on my raw skin. I'm a nervous wreck and the more aware of how anxious I am, the more nervous I get. It's really a miracle again that I got through any of this. It really is. But I know that I have been given a second chance, I know that I am on a mission for more than just myself and that I have a job to do. I don't question what, where, or how, I just do. I have been given the gift and shown to write. Write it out of my heart and mind and release it. Write it out to show where I am going and where I have been. Write it out in gratitude over and over because I am well aware that I am not doing this on my own, you can't. The pain is outside of human comprehension. I am giving thanks over and over for the things that I know to be for my future. I give thanks for the healing, happiness, and joyful thriving relationships with my daughters. I give thanks for it all because I know that I will receive it.

I know I need to get out on my own, I need to have my own place. I cannot listen to people tell me who I am, what I need, and how to do it because I am a mentally ill drug addict. It doesn't get any more enraging than having it come from you from all angles. Plus, I am the one who has done the work so I really see how sick and stuck other people are but are too consumed with telling me what is wrong with me, to worry about themselves. Everyone seems to think that they know better than I do myself. No wonder people take their own lives. Yes, I mean what I just said, 1000%. People get pushed and pushed when they are already down, to the point of no return. Listen, the old, learned understanding of what drug addiction and/or mental illness is wrong and outdated. If you want to be the reason for someone else's unwellness, then keep pushing. If you want to be a part of the solution, then please continue to listen and learn. And I am not saying this in a mean and belittling way because we don't know what we don't know. I have also been there. I beat myself up right alongside everyone else because I had those same old beliefs that they did. Again, that is why it is imperative to unlearn the crap that keeps us all sick and stuck. Anything small can and will eventually turn into something bigger, so do and learn this now. Enough of this mental health and addiction crisis. I really don't know what needs to happen for people to start to understand that it isn't someone else's problem or fault, it's ours and yours. There is no such thing as those bad people, in that bad neighborhood who do those bad things. Trust me, you all think that way until you actually acknowledge the way you think. We're all running on our preprogrammed thoughts that are old and outdated until they are not. The choice really is yours. The best way to change the world is to do an inside job, acknowledge your thoughts to change them, expand, and lead by example. When we all start leading by example in our own way, it allows others to do the same. Enough blaming the outside world for our problems. We will never change anything if we continue to do the same old learned way of doing things. You just have to know and understand what power you have when you take accountability for and of you.

CHAPTER ELEVEN

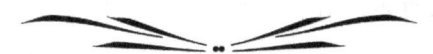

I need to move, and I need to move now. I know that I have to get away from everyone and everything, or I'm not going to be able to stay on track. It seems that everyone I know or the people who are willing to help me at this time, anyway, have their own struggles. I'm not here to judge, in fact, I don't judge. I know too much and have seen too much to judge anyone. I just know that I am in a very weak state and I'm trying to build myself back up. Even the people that I know who have stopped drinking and/or doing drugs, it doesn't mean that they can help me to get to where I am going. I'm not just removing the behaviors, I'm understanding why and healing, letting go, and getting rid of what no longer serves my higher purpose. I am pretty sure that the one-way conversations of me being told what I needed to do meant they still had their own journey to go on. These are the things that you learn and the awareness that you receive once you decide to heal and grow. To let go of all the things that you know, so you can know better.

I have to get my own place and I am going to take my ex back to court. I didn't have a say before. I had been told what to sign even though I said I was scared and didn't know or understand what I was signing.

Like I said, I found an attorney who would take me on and one that I felt somewhat comfortable with. I don't think it was him directly, I didn't really trust anyone. I would hire him to reopen the spousal support agreement and then custody 50/50 of the girls. The paperwork I had signed while I was in treatment said I agreed to 0 spousal support and for him to have 100% custody. I was bullied into signing those papers. I can understand logically, of course, he wanted to get on with his life. Emotionally, I was stuck for a very long time in my thoughts of why he wasn't there for me when I needed him the most, and why he didn't believe me. I must say it again that this is a question that I had to rid myself of. And I recommend that anyone who finds themselves in a situation where they are hurt by another, give it up. You will never find the answer to that question, you don't need it, and it's not going to help you even if you do have the answer. When we heal ourselves, we heal ourselves by letting all that is out of our control go. We don't have control over other people's actions nor should we ever try. You mind your business and allow others to do the same.

I would say it took about a year from when I got back from treatment, went through that whole weaning and the cold turkey of antipsychotics, got a job, and moved from where I was staying and got my own place. I got an attorney for spousal support, visitation changes, and, eventually, 50/50 custody. I had gone to try to talk to his attorney on my own without representation to ask for visitation changes, with no luck. I had to jump through hoops to see the girls at his will and whim. If I couldn't make it, I got called out on what a terrible and irresponsible mother I was. I was never asked how my health was, just blamed for not asking how high when I was told to jump. I share all of this to point out what our children bear witness to. They are very aware of how their parents treat each other. We are supposed to be the adults. We are the ones who when life becomes difficult and overwhelming show them that love will work it out respectfully. We don't show them that one parent matters more than the other. We don't feed them lies because we want to shelter them from the truth. One more time, we don't lie to them to shelter them from the truth. We work together when it's hard, so we aren't left alone trying to figure out what the truth really is. We don't create what will hinder us in our relationships later in life. We perpetuate the same in each generation that we don't heal. We repeat what we haven't learned and healed from. These are the reasons why our relationships struggle and fail later in life. If we don't have an example, or we get mixed messages about what a healthy relationship is, how do we have one of our own? And then we question ourselves on what we did wrong or what is wrong with the other person. Can't we see that we're all products of the same in one way or another? We have to work at it. We have to learn, heal, grow, and try to understand where each is coming from, even if we ourselves don't know. Blaming people for doing only what they know or have been taught is a losing battle.

Part of the visitation would be random drug testing. In the paperwork, I had found it said that I have an hour to get the test done when randomly selected.

I don't have a clue how they wanted this to actually happen. I was always in agreement with drug testing, but it also had to be realistic. It would be changed after going back and forth and back and forth with my now attorney that I hired. It was a joke for me to think I would get anywhere on my own. I agreed to the testing and would be given 2 hours. So I had to take time off work to get tested. My job was about a 40-minute drive from the testing place. I couldn't always have my phone on me so I would have to sneak into the break room to check on it periodically. Because in actuality I only had an hour and a half. And there are no excuses to be made. It doesn't matter if you have a job or where you live. It was made close to impossible for me to do. And any mistakes that are made are yours and only yours. If you're out of the time frame, it's processed as a dirty test, and I don't get to see my children. And yes, that happened, and by no fault of my own.

The first time it happened was when I was taking my doctor-prescribed Suboxon. They had randomly tested me around the same time, so it would show the same amount in my system. On one occasion they had notified me at a different time and I had taken one of my daily doses. Because it was higher than the previous, it was considered to be abuse of the medication, which I did not. Not once. After I got the help that I needed, I understood addiction and was clean and sober, that was it. I did not make any mistakes. So, right after the testing, it goes immediately into the system. The system that directly and, I swear, instantaneously notifies the attorney who notifies my ex. And of course, there is no explaining myself, how, why, and that I did nothing wrong. I don't get to see my girls. Nobody takes accountability, I just lose my time with my girls and them with me.

The second time was also not my fault. This time I got a random notification later in the day. I was a bit surprised but also thankful because I wouldn't have to leave work early and rush to get there. I walked into the place and up to the check-in window. It's one big waiting room with a counter and someone on the other side of the window who checks you in. So, it's one side waiting room, the other with about eight desks in the middle of this big room with a few offices behind the desks. I'm checking in at the window, and the lady behind the desk says, sorry you're late, you missed your appointment. I said, no way, look at my phone, it says right here. Again, I'm told I missed my appointment. Then, from across the entire room, the manager of the place yells at me so everyone in there can hear me getting yelled at. You missed it, nope, no excuses. Wait wait, no please look this is from your office, please look. Nope, you missed your appointment. I asked her to please get up and look at my phone to see, whether it was from their office. Nope, you should have known better. I am furious. I'm trying my hardest to control myself. I want to jump over the counter to kick this lady's ass. It was so ugly and unnecessary. And this is the manager of the place. It was as if she was waiting for the opportunity to belittle someone because she thought she could. She had the power whether or not I got to see my children. I excused myself and went outside.

Because I was in the process of going to court, I had an attorney. Never would I have had an attorney on call, but it just so happened that I did then. I called him and explained the situation. He said to go back in there and tell her that your attorney wants to talk to her. This is what made me so angry too. I walked in and yes, I was an asshole right back and on the top of my lungs, well maybe not that loud, I said my attorney wants to talk to you, now. Of course, she jumps up from her chair and walks over to me. With a smile on her face, she says, of course, no problem and reaches for my phone. It was such a gross display of who that person really was. It was like the flick of a switch. And she apologized for the confusion. There was no confusion, it was their mistake, and nobody would hold themselves accountable and put it on me because they could. The damage, of course, had already been done - automatic notification to the attorney that alerts my ex. I tried calling him to explain. He would not even talk to me. He just said that my attorney could talk to his attorney and that I would not be seeing the girls. I did not get to see the girls nor did the girls get to see their mother. Nobody thinks about their immediate actions and the cause and effect of all those affected by their actions. Your power trippin' has far-reaching consequences. I just don't understand. Why would you want to hurt somebody so bad that you don't even know, has nothing to do with you, that you know nothing about, and you are just assuming? And by assuming you are just making up this ugly story in your head and believe it as fact. Do you see what happens when you create an ugly story about someone else because you have your own unresolved issues? Every single one of us needs to heal in one way or another, or we are just as bad as those we think beneath us.

Eventually, and over a year of back and forth, stipulation this, stipulation that, random drug testing, jumping through hoops, and moving a few times (another long ass story), I won. I had spousal support for five years and 50/50 custody of the girls. I did it. The girls and I had said for years, "Our time will come," and it did. Our time would and did come but it would come at yet another big price. By this time now I've done all kinds of therapy, and I've been working hard. I have a new therapist who has diagnosed me with major depressive disorder, anxiety, and PTSD. And this is about the time when I would come to learn that my now ex-husband was a covert gaslighting narcissist. And so many things started to fall into place for me. All of those years of questioning myself started to make sense. WOW! So many things started to make sense. I really must say that this is not about bad-mouthing anyone but showing and giving you an understanding of what a narcissist is. And if I haven't said it before, I'll say it now. We are all products of this world and deserve to heal and live a fulfilling life. However, a covert narcissist can also be very dangerous. If you don't ever think you're doing anything wrong, what are your boundaries and limits to what you will say and do without taking accountability for your own actions? As I said, doing some research really helped me in the end. I had already done so much work but there was always something missing. This is one of the biggest and greatest things that I have learned and I hope whoever needs to hear this does as well. I stayed stuck for so long because I worked on fixing what I was being told was wrong with me. Think about that in your own life. Have you ever been told who you are and what you do wrong? If so, it's time to check that out. There is a difference between your behavior and the person you really are. I've seen it, how many of us are so afraid to actually look at ourselves because of what we have been told. We don't want to know the truth. We are afraid of the truth. But we don't have to be. The fear is made up of more lies and it is true. And our behavior can be changed once we acknowledge the reason. We really do all win.

CHAPTER TWELVE

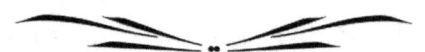

There was a lady in treatment I befriended when I was down south, in the dual diagnosis facility. When we'd sit in groups, I would mention things just like I would mention in conversation with anybody. And she'd always lean over to me and say, gaslighting. Gaslighting whenever I was talking about my now ex-husband, and I never knew what in the hell she meant because I'm not in a very good head space, I'm just not healthy. So you know, I'm still questioning my sanity and, obviously, now hers as well because I have no idea why she keeps leaning over to me and says, gaslighting, every time I talk about my now ex-husband. So, I would hear stories in there and they would kind of sound familiar, but it still didn't register. It took me to be so far removed from him to heal, then to start co-parenting to start to figure it all out. When I no longer had to listen to him tell me or dictate when I would see the girls and I had my own voice to use. So there I was again questioning my own sanity. I knew that something was wrong and I had a new therapist, and we were talking about my entire, well, experience. So she was the one, I believe, who pretty much drove it home for me. Telling me who he was. That still does not make it easy to deal with. And trying to co-parent was a nightmare. When you are finding yourself, getting yourself back, and then realizing who this person is and was, who this person was all along. You had to come full circle, to realize that you were the one who told the truth from the very beginning. You were the one who had asked for help but got ignored. Or asked for help and was told that you were treated like a queen and that all you do is complain. So, in return, I would question myself. I would question myself and think that I had been making all of it up. How do you even wrap your head around that? Well, you can't and I didn't and that's exactly why I snapped. I really was sick and had been telling the truth all along. I had questioned my sanity and the person I was time and time and again but always gave him the benefit of the doubt. I thought so little of myself that his opinion of me mattered more than my own. I had completely lost myself. I almost gave up because I believed what I was being told. I thought I was making up being sick so I could do drugs. When I said I am not bipolar, please don't make me take this medication, I was told you're either bipolar or you're a really bad person. I believed that and I was neither. I believed everything that I was being told and I almost gave up. It's still difficult to think about this time in my life and wonder if it was as bad as I thought it was. And the answer to that is, it is a miracle that I am alive. The only reason I am even alive today is by the grace of God. Had he not reached his hand out to me when I was trying to hide from him, I would not be alive today. My own thoughts could not comprehend what was going on. I needed a supernatural kind of help. It is a vicious cycle when you don't understand what you don't understand. When you can't make sense of any of your thoughts, you're lost. And when you're lost, it is very difficult to make wise or healthy choices. You don't even know that you have choices. You're just doing and hoping for the best. If nothing is logical, how do you make logical choices? Plus, just because you go to treatment doesn't mean you're going to get the help you need. It's individual treatment, so being labeled and put in a box just keeps the cycle going.

Besides doing the traditional talk therapy with my new therapist, I was still searching for more. It wasn't enough because I was trying to heal from the same thing that I was having to deal with, trying to co-parent. It's like getting help for PTSD while you're out on the battlefield. I would get triggered over and over. However, while I did the work with my therapist I also did my own research. I had to understand what a narcissist's traits are. I could start to see and understand what I did not before. I just took everything as a *me* problem because, basically, I was being told to do so. I was being told so when I was already in such a weak state so I believed it. When I reflect back though now, it was so obvious. Had I been in my right mind I would have responded differently. But then you have to wonder how I got into the relationship, to begin with. Well, I have the answer to that now too. I got into an unhealthy relationship because I was unhealthy, to begin with. Like so many of us really are. We have to acknowledge who we are as a whole person to understand who we really are. That means doing the work. I was such an insecure person deep down. I didn't think I really mattered unless I was married with children. I would not be whole or complete unless I was at least married. Really, I just wanted to be loved and accepted.

With all the different modalities, self-help, and therapy, this was also the time when I started to do some more digging and to do the deep work. There is a lot to be said about childhood trauma, and we all have it. This is exactly why I encourage others to not see mental health or illness as somebody else's issue or problem but to also see it in themselves as well. Mental health isn't scary until it is, so don't go there. We are all products of this world, and we all need to heal from it in one way or another. If you find yourself struggling in any way with money, career, relationships, etc., it's time to do the inside job. I believe, well no, I know what is keeping so many of us stuck and in repeating patterns and unaware at the same time. It is all the things we" think we know." When we stay so stuck in what "we think we know," it gets in the way of knowing more. And yes, you can and are probably right on how and why you are so angry at any given situation. But what you are unaware of is how to get yourself out. You've been in the situation or had the problem for so long that that is all you know and has become your normal. Can you see again how these things are not your fault and nothing to be ashamed of or afraid of? We make up stories because we've heard it over and over about why we should fear a situation but that doesn't make it so. It was taught to you to keep you from seeking out what you are entitled to. And when I say entitled, it's not snot-nosed, I deserve something over someone else kind of attitude. No one matters more than someone else. And maybe that's the first check-in with yourself you can do. How do you really feel about other people? Do you think you matter more than others and if so why. Remember there is a cause and effect that has no bounds to your behavior, so we all have to pay attention to the bigger picture. We've been taught to be small-minded when we think we matter more than others. It's actually an ugly way of being and will eventually keep you stuck in a scarcity mindset. And that means there will come a time when limits will be put on you and everything that you do. You will not be able to find peace or the next level, because we stay stuck with our limitations in the way we think about things. Drop the ego so you can expand your mind. It's time for us to make our own individual choices for change.

And when I say change, I mean the kind that has a great impact on generations to come. Which side do you prefer to be on? You might not yet believe you have such power, but I am telling you that you do. As soon as you believe you can go after it. The most powerful stand we can make is the one we make to be ourselves. Stop trying so hard to be someone you are not, so you can allow what is meant for you to be.

So, along with the EMDR (Eye movement and desensitization and reprocessing therapy, good for people with PTSD) I also did some anger releasing, if you will. In therapy, I was given a baseball bat and a heavy bag and was told to yell out all of my anger while wailing on the bag. What an awesome release. For all of those people who hurt me, hurt my children, took my children away from me in one way or another. I hit that bag so fucking hard that I could barely hold on because my hands hurt so bad. I was screaming and crying by the end of it. My whole body and face were buzzing. It was and is something I recommend for anyone and everyone to do. No holding onto the shit that has hurt you. That negative energy doesn't belong in your body. It's not yours to hold onto or to keep, so release it.

All the therapy was good, yes, I needed it. I needed all of the help in the world. When the world is barking at you like a rabid dog, you need help. I was getting help for the obvious things while life was still happening. I had two more emergency trips to the hospital, Covid happened, and the accumulation of having to take time off for random drug tests and health reasons would have me lose my job. I was told I was welcome back at any time, once I got back on my feet. I wasn't quite there with my new way of thinking, but for the most part, I saw it as a gift. The old me would have panicked wondering what I would do, but I had new tools to use. My new tools were a new way of thinking. I could relax, remember, and know that all things are always working out for my best. Even though I didn't have a job and it worried me that my ex might find out and try to take the children away, I got real with myself. I thought long and hard about the fact that he could not hurt me unless I allowed him to. When I stayed strong and stood up for myself, he might still have some nasty things to say but that was on him not me. I didn't care anymore, what he had to say, because I knew it wasn't true. And when you get prepared and ahead of it, knowing how he will respond and act in certain situations, you stay grounded. I'm no longer shocked, outraged, or take offense. He can no longer hurt me. I know who he is. I'm not an expert at it but, for the most part, I don't have to concern myself on why he behaves the way that he does. I actually give him some grace and remember where he comes from. It's learned and taught behavior. I'm never going to change him, so the only thing I can do is change myself. Yes, it does take work, but I know not to take my guard down. Like I said before I just have to get ahead of it and prepare myself. If I know I will have to talk to him or co-parent in some way, I get prepared. When I don't prepare, I get hurt. But the difference now, is I know how to turn it around and not be offended by it. Or I might be at first but I have the tools and the insight into that behavior to turn it around. A situation that used to leave me bedridden and questioning my very existence. Not anymore and never again.

In the back of my mind, this knowing was what kept me grounded. The knowing without the knowing, having faith that everything that I had asked for would happen and work out for me. I have had an unwavering faith in that even when I didn't. I still had my moments when the old habits of thinking I have to "DO" would show up, but then I went back to my tools. I went back to my writing. I went back and saw that from the very beginning, everything was working out exactly the way that I had asked for it to work out.

After losing my job, initially, I freaked out, I crawled up in a ball and went to bed, and then I was totally relieved and grateful. Like I said before, I had a new way of thinking and a new mindset, I was a different person, and now was the time to put it to the test. I knew everything was going to be OK and that everything always works out for my greater good but I had to get in my own way again. Even though I had that sense of peace and relief in knowing all this, the old "doing" showed up. Seriously, again.

I thought OK, it's a blessing I don't have to force myself to go to this job because I'm still not healthy and I'm making myself OK. I had made myself OK for everyone else though. I had to jump through the hoops, so I could get the girls back. I had to have all the things on the outside that made the impression that I had it all together again. And that meant I had to show up the way they wanted me to, not in the real way I was thinking or feeling. Whatever, I knew my time would come. I knew my time would come when I would no longer have to show up in any other way than just being me.

So, this is the time that I am reflecting back on everything that has happened to me and in my favor. I am so grateful. I have my girls back 50/50, living now in the condo that I bought with our family dog that we said we would get "when our time comes." It really is a miracle. But once again, it was too good to be true, so I got back in my own way yet again and said, "OK, God you obviously want me to do something. Whatever you want, I'm going to prove myself to you." I wanted to show how thankful I was for, well, every single thing he did. Without divine intervention, this wouldn't have happened. On one hand, and this is hilarious, I said, "OK God, you want me to become a nun." I have to laugh so hard at that now. I even said to God, no way. I mean, yes of course, if that's what you want but nobody is ever going to take me seriously. I mean that's the biggest joke ever, but OK, you know best. Thank goodness I got out of that thought process. What was I even thinking? Actually, well, I'll get to that in a second. So the next thing I did was sign up for Christian businesses x, y, and z. I won't name the companies or the programs, but they were definitely not my jam. I was trying so hard to find my people, listen to God, and start my own business, you see where I'm going with this. But time and time again, I failed. I failed because they were forcing an agenda, an agenda that was the opposite of what God had been trying to show me all along. God didn't want to change me. God didn't want me to change myself. God wanted me to see myself as the person I really am and have always been and to love myself for that. To love myself unconditionally for all the good, the bad, and the ugly. To love myself just as he loves me. One and the same. He showed me the opposite of what religion was trying to teach me. He showed me that we all have a connection to him because we are him. We are the one-of-a-kind individual that nobody else can be. And that we all are. Our limitations are all man-made, not God-made. So, when we get rid of the man-made baggage we get a connection to a limitless source of abundance in every aspect of our lives. When we make the decision to cut the crap and lead with our hearts and then our minds, that's when real life begins. We get to wake up every morning excited for the opportunities that are to come our way. When we are on our path, we've already created where we are going. Live in the mindset of endless possibilities because it is so. You don't have to worry about how you're going to get there, you just take the steps there. The path is to go out in this world and live it. The steps will present themselves when you believe faithfully that the next step will be presented to you. It is the removal of fear and questioning, to make room for allowing and receiving. If you worry, you stand in the way. So, get rid of the ego that says it knows better to allow what is better to come to you. Our ego is all of the learned crap that we no longer need. Our ego might have helped us once upon a time, we might have needed it to survive. But guess what, you've survived. You did it, now it's time to use what you've learned along the way to help those who need it. That goes for you, me, and everybody else who wants to make progressive change in this world. It's happening anyway, so jump, what are you waiting for?

CHAPTER THIRTEEN

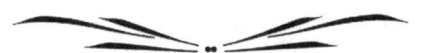

This is the work I wish everyone would do. To realize and understand that "normal" was not necessarily normal growing up. It's just how it was. I know for myself I grew up at a time when there was no such thing as depression. It was you-got-a-problem-fix-it, when you can't, it's "a you" problem, so you suck it up and stuff it down.

There were so many things I just did not know that I know now. And I know that goes for so many of us. So don't be afraid to see who you really are. There is nothing to fear. We only fear it because of the mixed messaging we've gotten growing up in this world.

When I started to do more of the work that I knew I needed to do on myself, that's when I really started to heal and wake up. When I say wake up, I mean to the person I have always been under the layers of crap. We all reside under the layers that need to be pulled back. And we have to pull them back because it's not about the obvious things. The obvious are the surface behaviors, not what needs to be healed. And when I say heal, I mean released, and I'll show a practice to do so you can get started right after reading this. Think of it this way. We don't know what gets trapped along with the major and obvious things or events that happen to us. When we only do the superficial stuff we still don't get to release it all. And superficial doesn't mean that it's not important, I just mean that it's obvious that you need to heal from it. I have had some sexual abuse and those are what I mean by the obvious and surface level. Do you see what I mean? When we only take those larger things into consideration, then we miss all of the smaller accumulation of things, and some of the behaviors because of the larger ones. And the behaviors get labeled as bad without an understanding of the root cause and effect. My parents also got divorced when I was around eight, and my mom went back home to Germany so I would get shuffled around. I would listen to my other family members bad-mouth my mom for leaving me and going back to Germany. And things aren't always so easy and black and white, so I always understand that my mom was not an American so why would she stay here after divorce? And my dad wouldn't let her take me anyway. I also didn't know that abandonment is not just people leaving you but also you leaving them. It was my "norm" to go back to Germany to see my family and then to have to leave them again, and again, and again. And when I was home here in the States, kids would make jokes about me being a Nazi and my family being Nazis. I didn't really know the impact that had had on me. But I did always wonder why the people that I love most in this world would be called such monsters. Even though I knew it wasn't true, you still picked up on some mixed messages without even being aware. So, I'm not going to get into my whole childhood and my understanding around it, that's a whole other story and not meant for what this book is about. I wrote this book because once upon a time I lost my voice. I could not advocate for myself and I did not matter. And my experience wasn't just an isolated event that only affected me. And my story even though its own, has many similarities to what other people can and do go through and experience in this world. In fact I have seen it firsthand. Had I not pushed through the fear of getting to know the real me, this book would have never been written. In fact, I stayed stuck in not doing it because of my fear. I also realized that it was a fear and one that I could heal from if I just got out of my own way and my thoughts around it all. We are our own worst enemy because of " what we think we know". We're stubborn basically. I know I was. I was afraid of being wrong. It's so easy and so hard at the same time.

And that's what brings me to here and now and what I want to share with you. For the most part, we've been taught that by doing more, we achieve more, we are more, more, more, more. The whole pushing ourselves to success road map. This is the enemy of all things and growth. We push ourselves into a corner. When we stay stuck it's because we think we have it all figured out because we played by the rule book. The rule book is old, limiting, and outdated.

So, I want to ask you to do a simple exercise. It's something that I have done and continue to do.

I was given a "download," if you will. I was basically shown to just write. To "thought dump". That means to not have an agenda and just start writing. Just sit down and write without a thought of what you think you "need" to write or what you "should" write.

This is how we uncover what is on our subconscious mind and what we need to rid ourselves of. It is also a way of communing with our higher self. It is a connection to something bigger than just ourselves. You have so much experience already. You've done so much learning. You've had a career and relationships. You've done a lot. Now it's time to take it all to another level. When we do this simple exercise, we build and grow into the person that we really are. We get to let go of what no longer has anything to do with here and now. Do you see the profound change that can be made just by telling yourself to shut the hell up and get out of the way? We, humans, will sabotage what seems to be too easy because we are accustomed to pushing and doing everything the hard way. I ask that you just give it a try.

Sit down and do a thought dump for three minutes then put it away. Try it again the following day and put it away. Try different combinations of it and then go back and read it. What do you see? Who was that person? What seems to come up more than other things? What are the repetitive negative patterns and self-talk? When we see the negative, we can flip that and turn it into a positive affirmation. Start thinking about what you want, not what you don't have, and write that out. Write everything out until the negative starts to turn into the positive. We really do have choices to completely change our lives as soon as we acknowledge what is really on our minds. Not what we think is on our minds, but what is really on our minds. Sometimes, we only think we're good people making good decisions and doing good things until we uncover what our subconscious programming is actually thinking and doing. And that's not your fault. But it is your choice to change it. We have the capacity to make great changes in this world when we do the individual inside job. That means taking accountability for who you really are with no limits or excuses. When you do that, you lead by example and that is how we change the world.

CONCLUSION

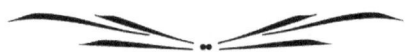

I am well aware that this isn't the best book you've ever read but I hope that the message will be received. I have written this so many times, rewritten, questioned, and second-guessed I'm surprised I finished it at all. It was too much, too little, not enough, etc., etc., etc. Any kind of self-defeating self-talk I could muster up, I was on it in full force. I allowed my fear to get the best of me. But I recognized the fear this time, understood where it was coming from, and I looked at it head-on. It was different this time. This was part of the process. This is where I got to acknowledge and make a conscious decision to step into my highest and best self. I had arrived.

And then I think about the time that I only existed in the paperwork that I dragged around in a bag from place to place. I got laughed at and called a bag lady, but no one really asked me what I was doing. No one could hear me, and no one asked. That bag had all the paperwork, the little paper doll cutouts, and medical records that I saved because I knew one day they would save me. Whenever I had any moments of clarity I wrote it down. That bag "of stuff" helped me remember who I was when I could not remember myself.

If you've ever been so afraid that you couldn't move or continue, then you will hear these words now. Stepping into the fear and doing it anyway. Taking a leap of faith. Know that this is just the beginning. These are and were the biggest steps that I had to make for myself. To let go of the fear of what might happen. I released everything that has ever held me back from becoming the person I am meant to be. This is also to show you the road it takes to get to where you are going. It's not perfect; in fact, it's messy. You make mistakes along the way, you question everything, but you do it anyway. If I wait for a perfect solution that will never come, then I lose. We all lose, really. You have to be willing to get out there and make mistakes and show that you are a human being. This isn't about the old way of doing things. This is about showing up as you are and continuing to grow from there. We waste so much time in our heads trying to prove ourselves while life passes us by. The more chances I take the better I get. The more mistakes I make the more I learn and grow. I will never go back to my old way of being. I will never allow anyone to tell me who I am. I will show you. I will show you and lead by example. And the road to real success is the truthful one.

The story was meant to show you that not all things are as they look, so don't make assumptions. Every single one of us is going through something so remember that next time before you judge. Mental illness and addiction are two of the biggest problems we have in this world and we still point the finger at everyone else before we hold ourselves accountable. We the people are the direct cause of the pain that this world feels and continues to inflict. We are all well aware of the problems in this world, but we do nothing to change it. And when I say change it, I mean doing the inside job. Until you can recognize and stand up wholeheartedly, with conviction of who you are and what you stand for, then you are just like everyone else. You are a part of the problem until you become the individual solution.

We all have our place in this world. And that means taking accountability for your life. I didn't get into great detail in this book but while I wrote this I had to lock myself away. I had to get away from it all. I had to know and understand the real me. And that means even when people have good things to say to you. Is that really you? I needed to know who I was, not who others told me I was, good or bad. And that should go for all of us. It's about getting real and honest with yourself.

Watching the news, complaining to your neighbors, and doing nothing different is not normal. Yelling at someone to get their shit together when they are sick is not normal. Just getting through things without actually healing is not normal. Thinking that you matter more than someone else is not normal or it shouldn't be. It should be common sense and a way of being, yet it's not.

So, my question to you is this. Who are you and who are you really? Do you push yourself to fit the image that others have created for you to be? Or are you standing up authentically as the person you were created to be? Be honest. I will tell you this. When you do, you will know true freedom. The walls and barriers will crumble. What is meant for you will come to you. And there is no comparison or competition. It is a place of peace, power, and purpose. We all have our own unique purpose. It doesn't mean you have to find the cure for cancer. Your purpose is to weed through the man-made illusion of fear to stand up as the one and only individual you are created to be. To love, respect, and understand yourself so others can do the same. We are angered because people can't show up the way they told us they would when they themselves didn't know that they couldn't. We have to change to change. Will that be you? The one that stands to heal generational trauma, to heal the past present, and the future. Every single one of us has that power as soon as we heal whatever it is that keeps us from it.

If you are still striving, pushing, and trying so hard then you are not in alignment with who you really are. So, who are you and who are you really?

We are in this together. Cheers to you for discovering who you really are and what you're capable of.

www.jessica-summers.com
Info@jessica-summers.com

ABOUT THE AUTHOR

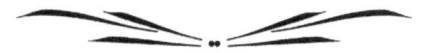

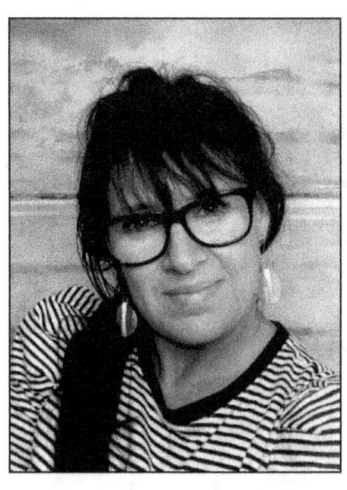

Jessica Summers is a distinguished speaker, consultant, and author renowned for her work in empowering high-achieving Gen X individuals to transcend personal and professional challenges. With a unique blend of personal experience and professional expertise, she has dedicated her life to helping others find peace, purpose, and power.

Drawing from her own journey of overcoming profound loss and adversity, Jessica inspires audiences worldwide with her transformative insights and practical wisdom. Her powerful storytelling and relatable approach make her a sought-after speaker at conferences, workshops, and events focused on women's empowerment and personal growth.

Passionate about spiritual growth, Jessica is also developing a course and journal to guide individuals on their spiritual journeys, encouraging them to surrender to their higher selves and embrace a life of authenticity and fulfillment.

When she's not working she's living life on her terms. Life is meant to be enjoyed, explored and preserved without limitations.

Connect with Jessica

Website:

www.jessica-summers.com

info@jessica-summers.com

Social Media:

https://www.facebook.com/profile.php?id=100080486230656&mibextid=LQQJ4d

http://linkedin.com/in/jessica-summers-b12680182

CONTINUE ON YOUR OWN JOURNEY : LET'S STAY CONNECTED

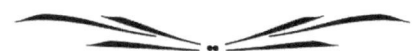

Thank you for reading "The Road to Now: From Tragedy to Triumph." Your journey towards peace, purpose, and power is just beginning. Here is how we can continue this transformative journey together:

1. **Hire Me as a Speaker:** Inspire and empower your audience by booking me for your next event. My keynotes and workshops are designed to spark profound change and growth. www.jessica-summers.com

2. **Work with Me:** Ready to take your personal or professional life to the next level? Let's collaborate through personalized coaching and consulting sessions tailored to your unique needs. www.jessica-summers.com

3. **Stay Connected on Social Media:** Follow me on LinkedIn and Facebook for daily insights, motivation, and updates. Stay inspired and engage with a community committed to growth.

    http://linkedin.com/in/jessica-summers-b12680182

    https://www.facebook.com/profile.php?id=100080486230656&mibextid=LQQJ4d

4. **Stay Updated with Upcoming Events:** Don't miss out on my latest workshops, webinars, and live events. Visit my website for all the details and to stay informed about new opportunities. www.jessica-summers.com

Your next chapter starts now. Let's elevate together!

www.ingramcontent.com/pod-product-compliance
Lightning Source LLC
Chambersburg PA
CBHW071020120626

46546CB00003B/1166